Glimpses of
a Feather
~ Mandalas ~

Jean A Williams

ISBN:1548167584
ISBN-13: 978-1548167585

DEDICATION

This book is dedicated to all of those people who helped me find my way from that point where I wondered why I wanted my life to continue, to the realization that my contributions mattered. You are all incredibly dear to me, and I am blessed for your part in my life.

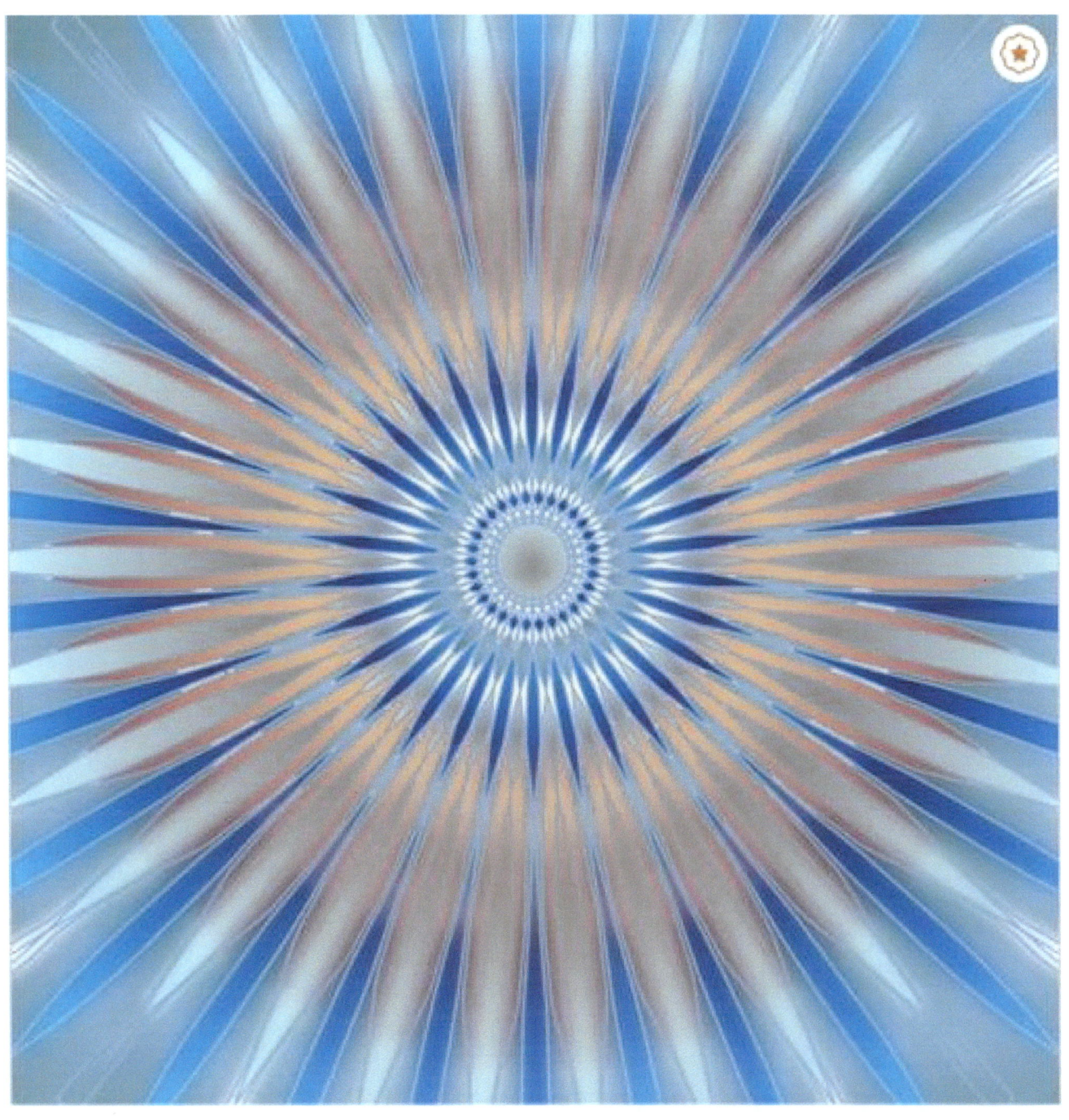

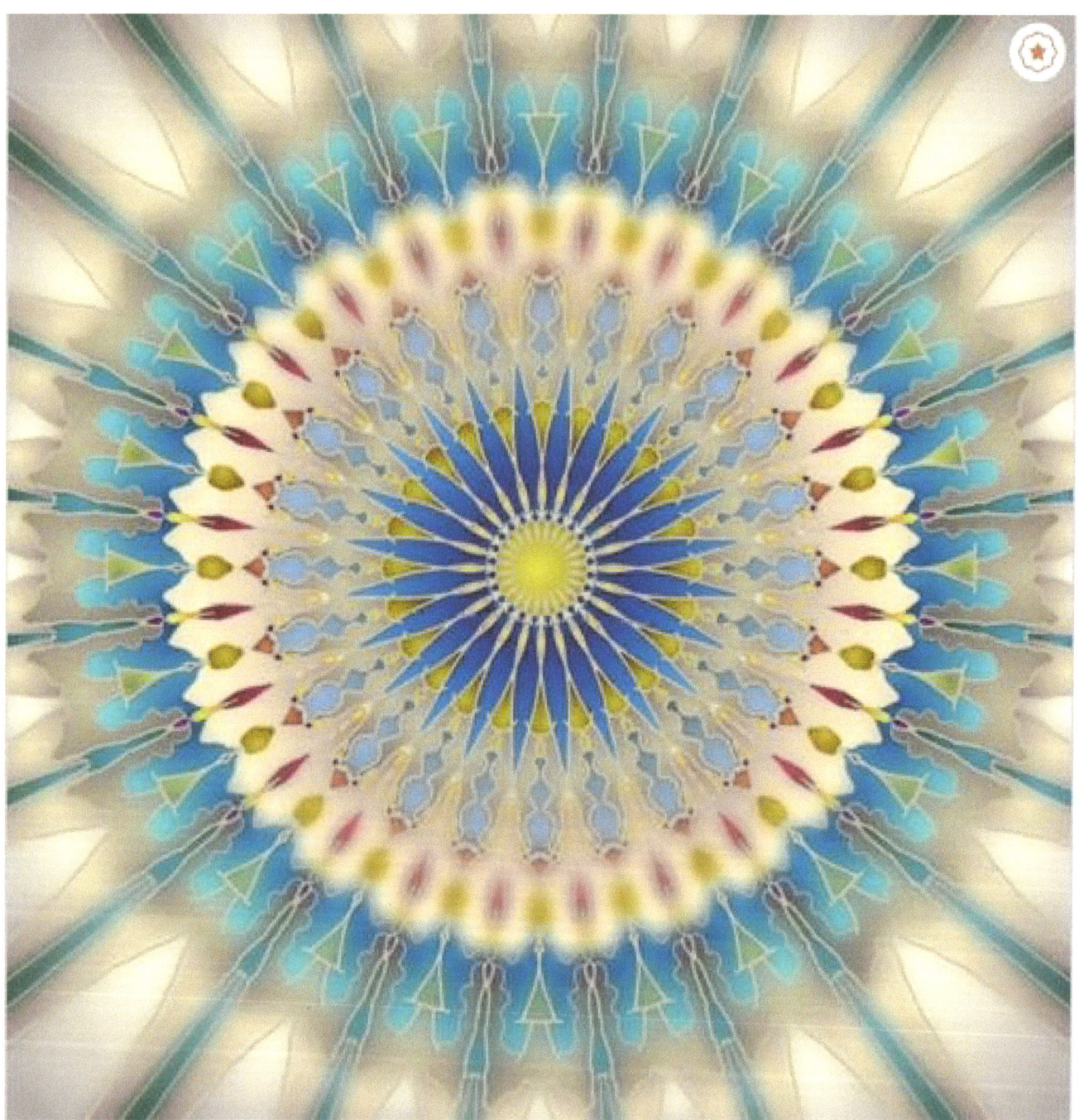

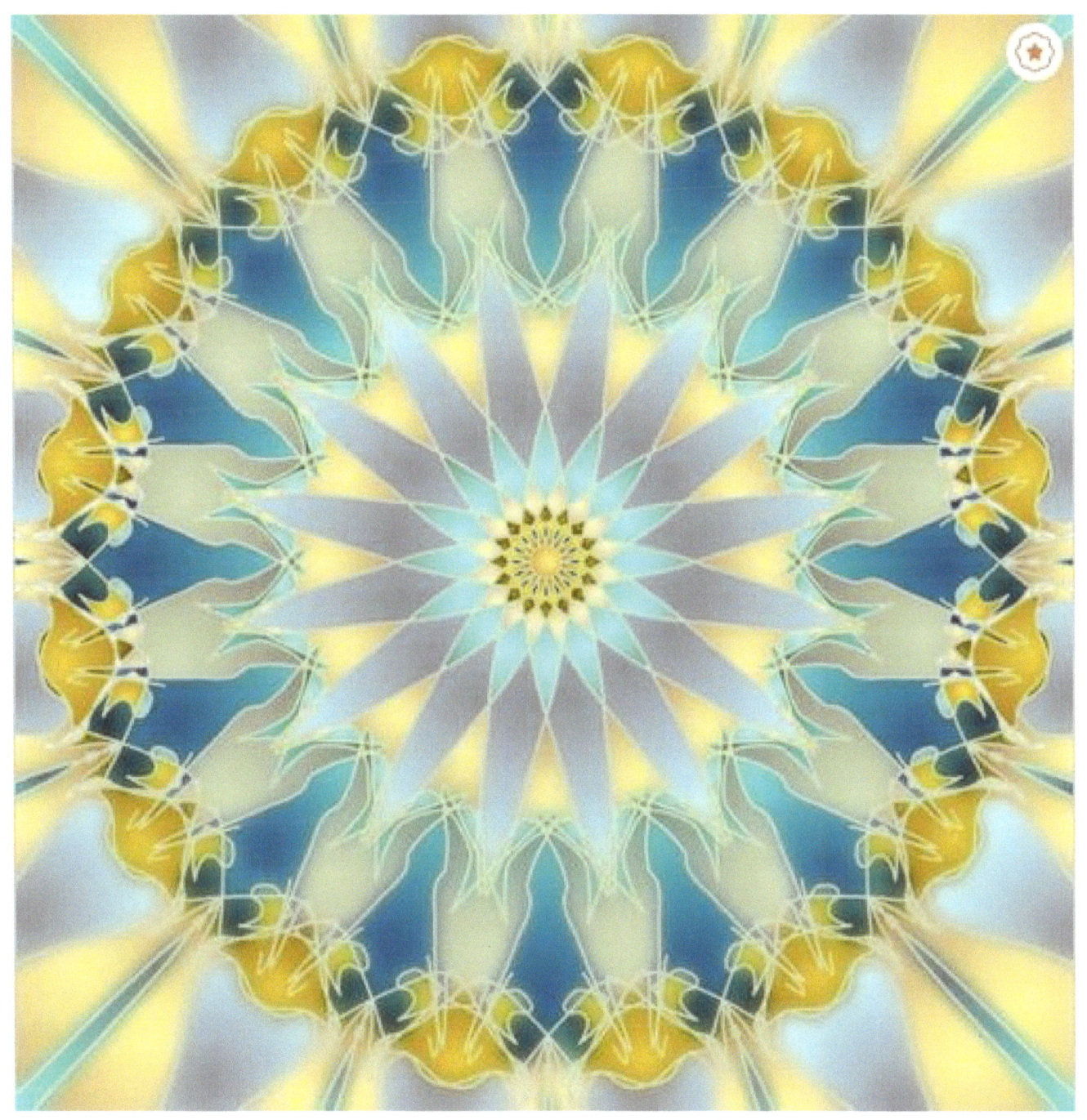

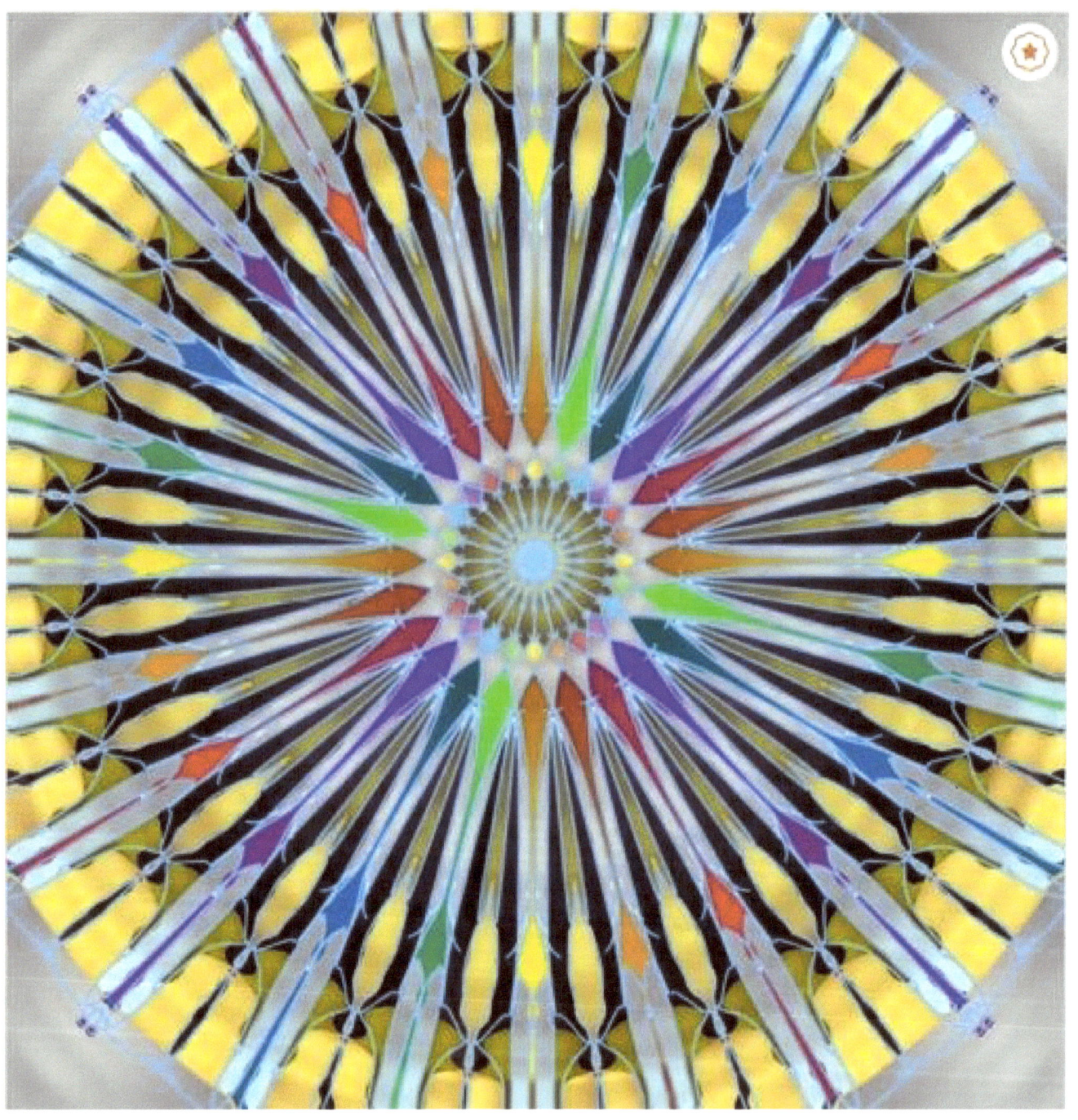

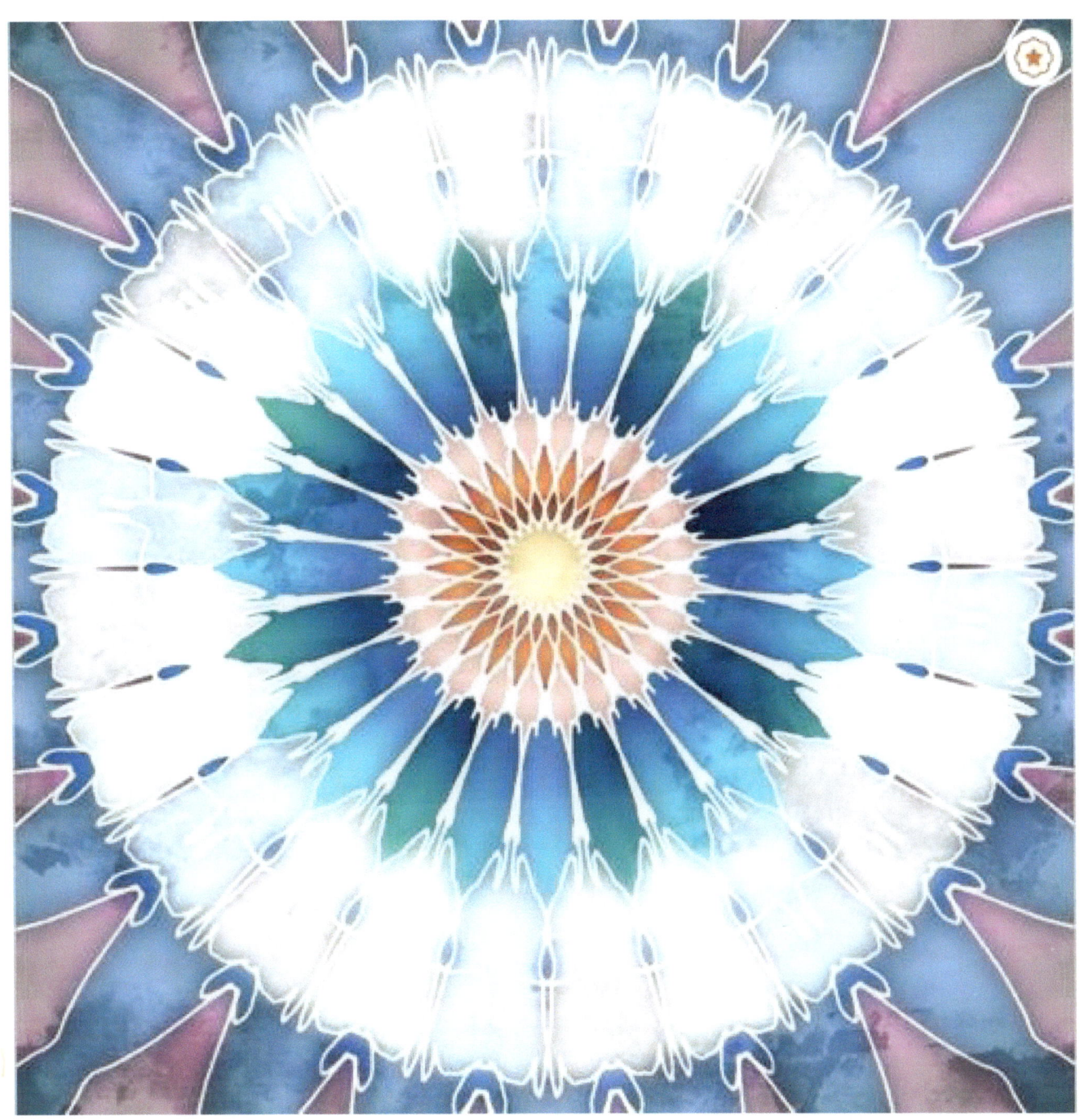

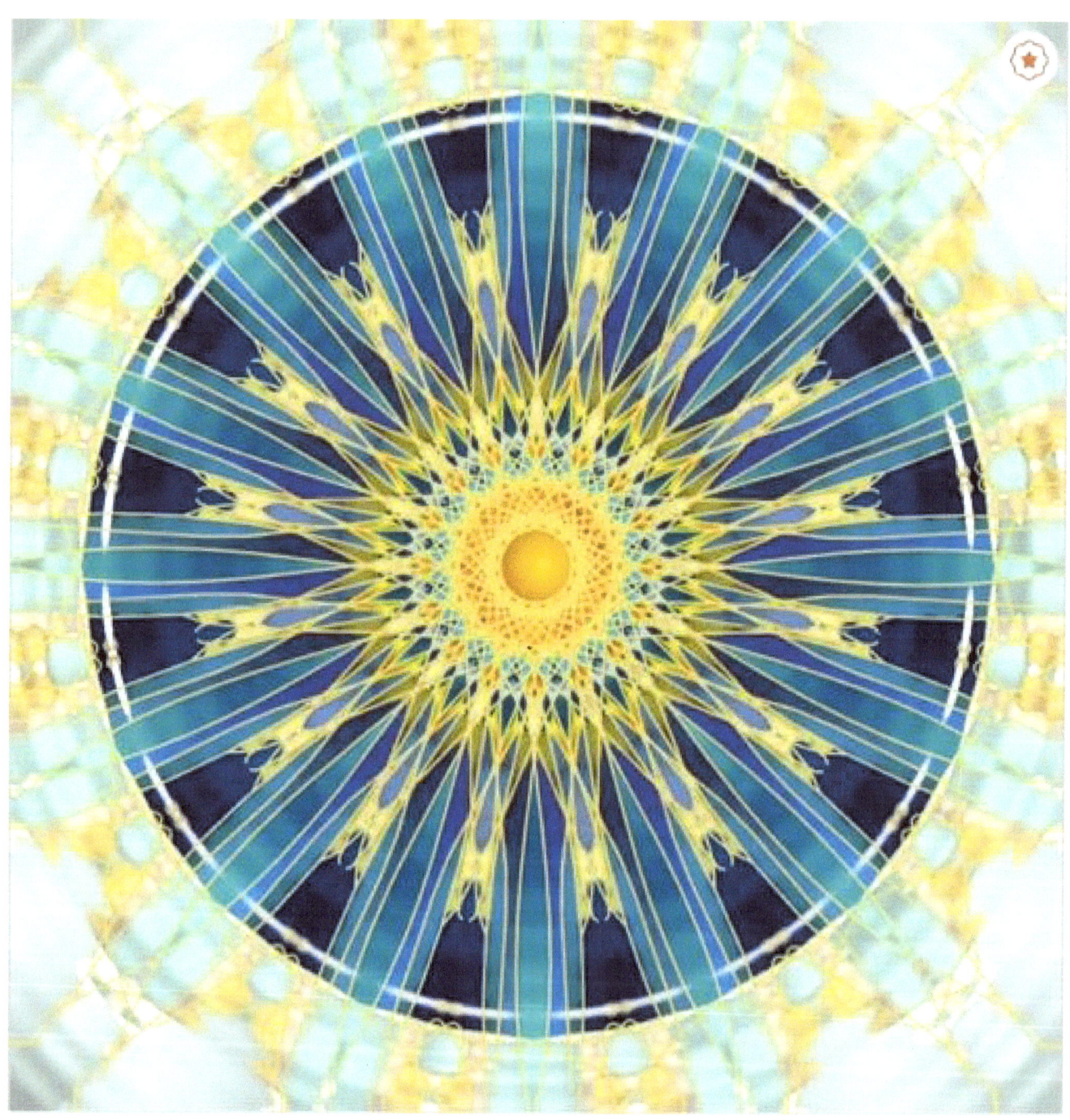

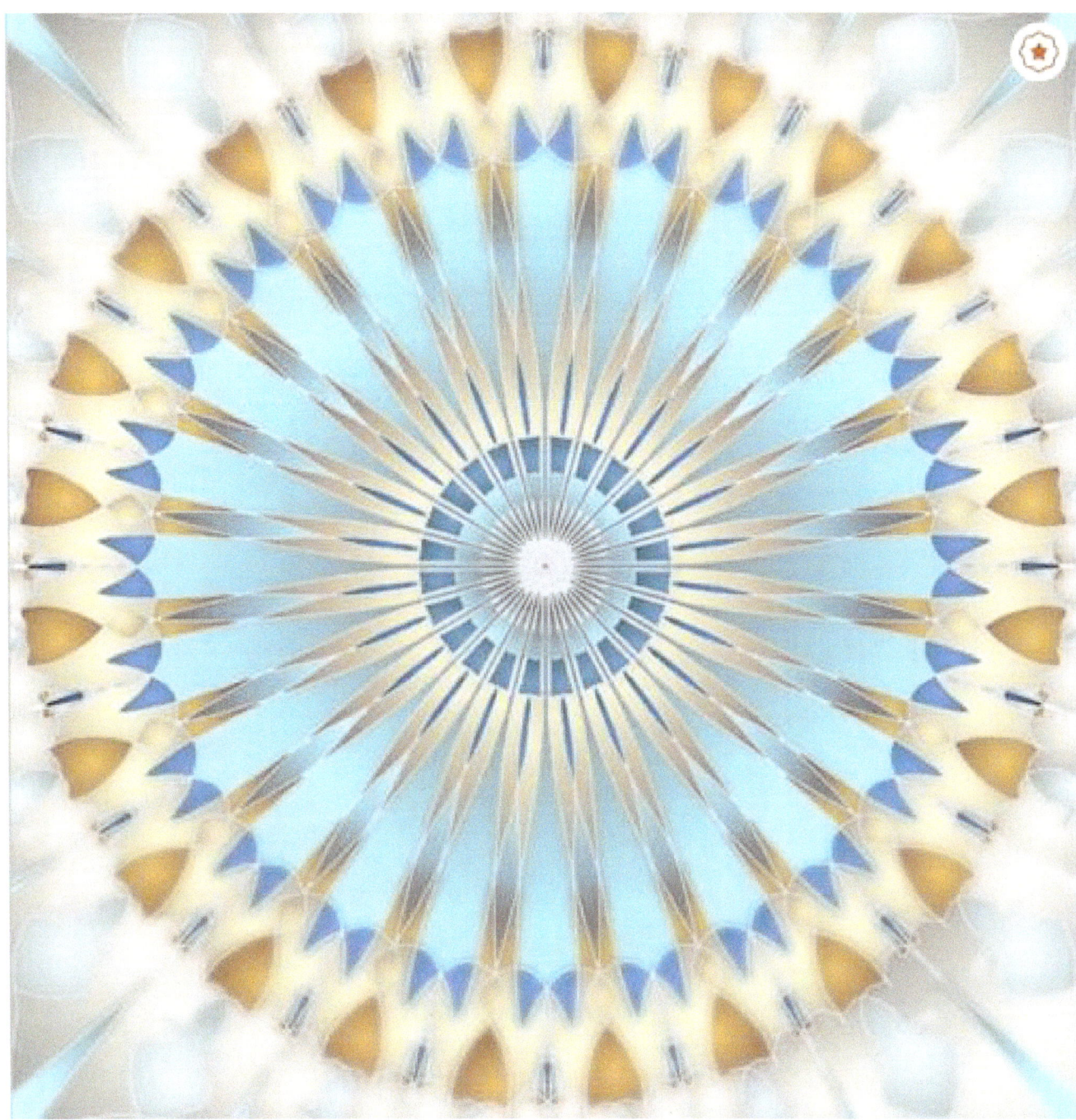

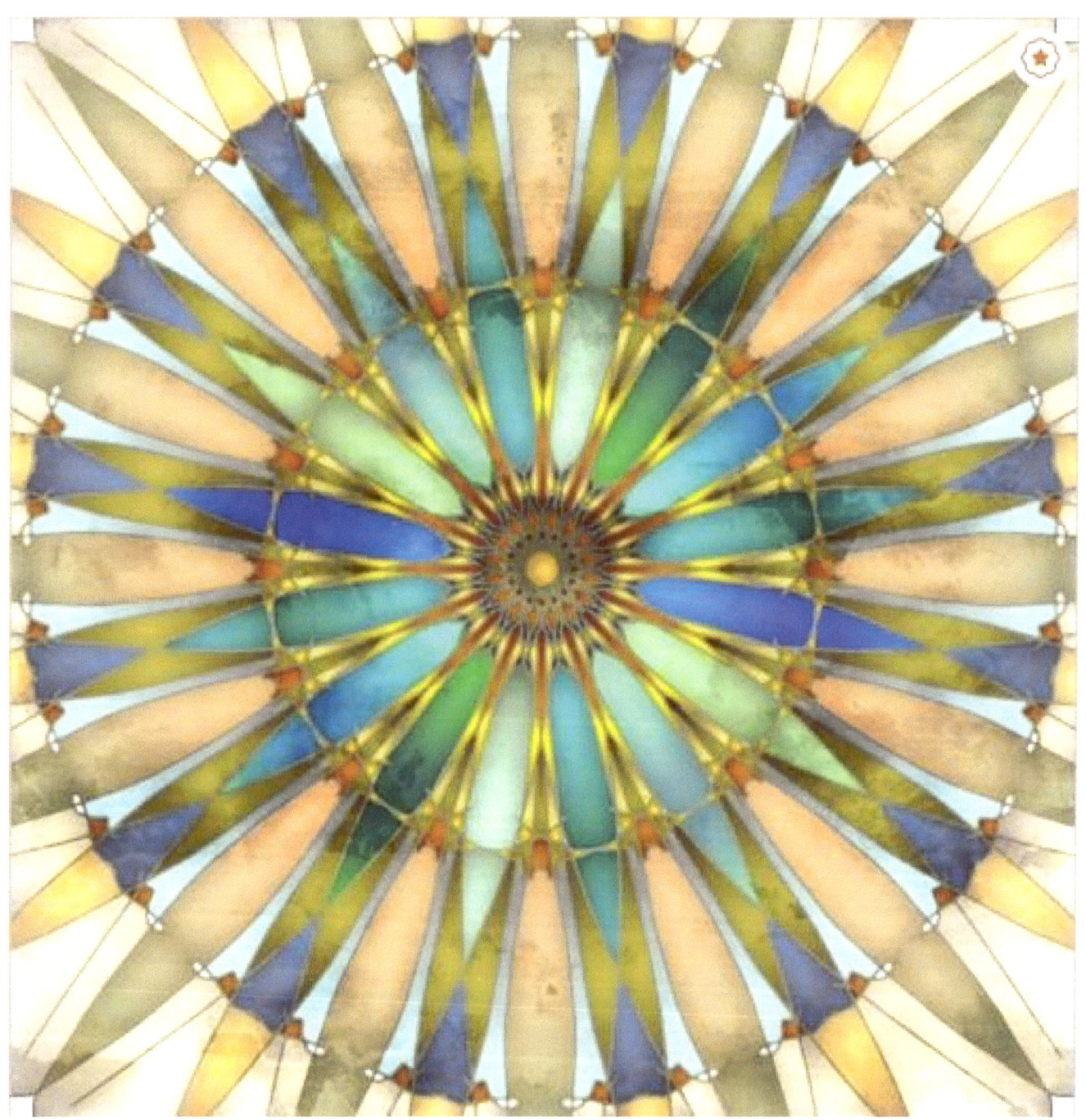

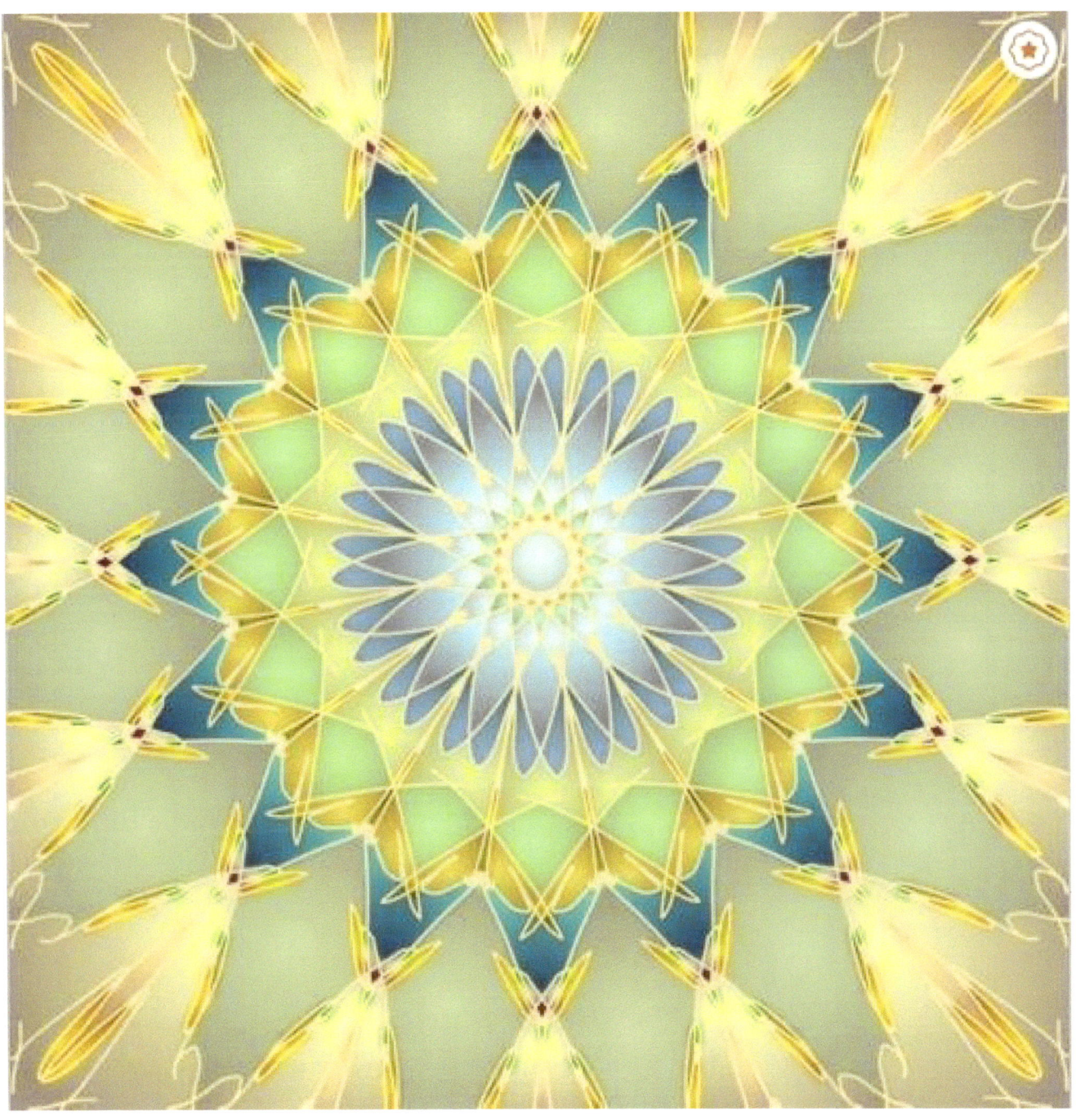

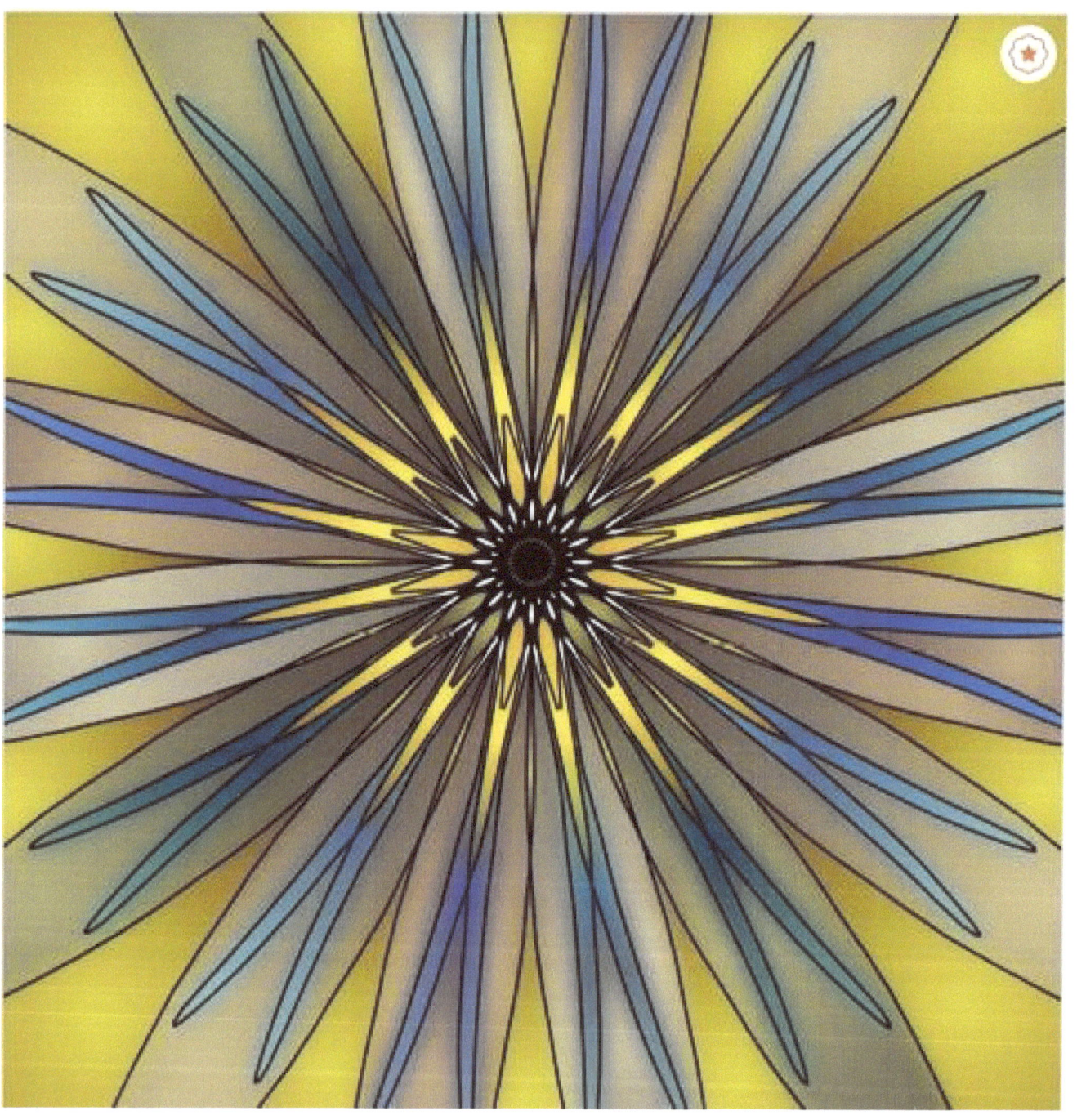

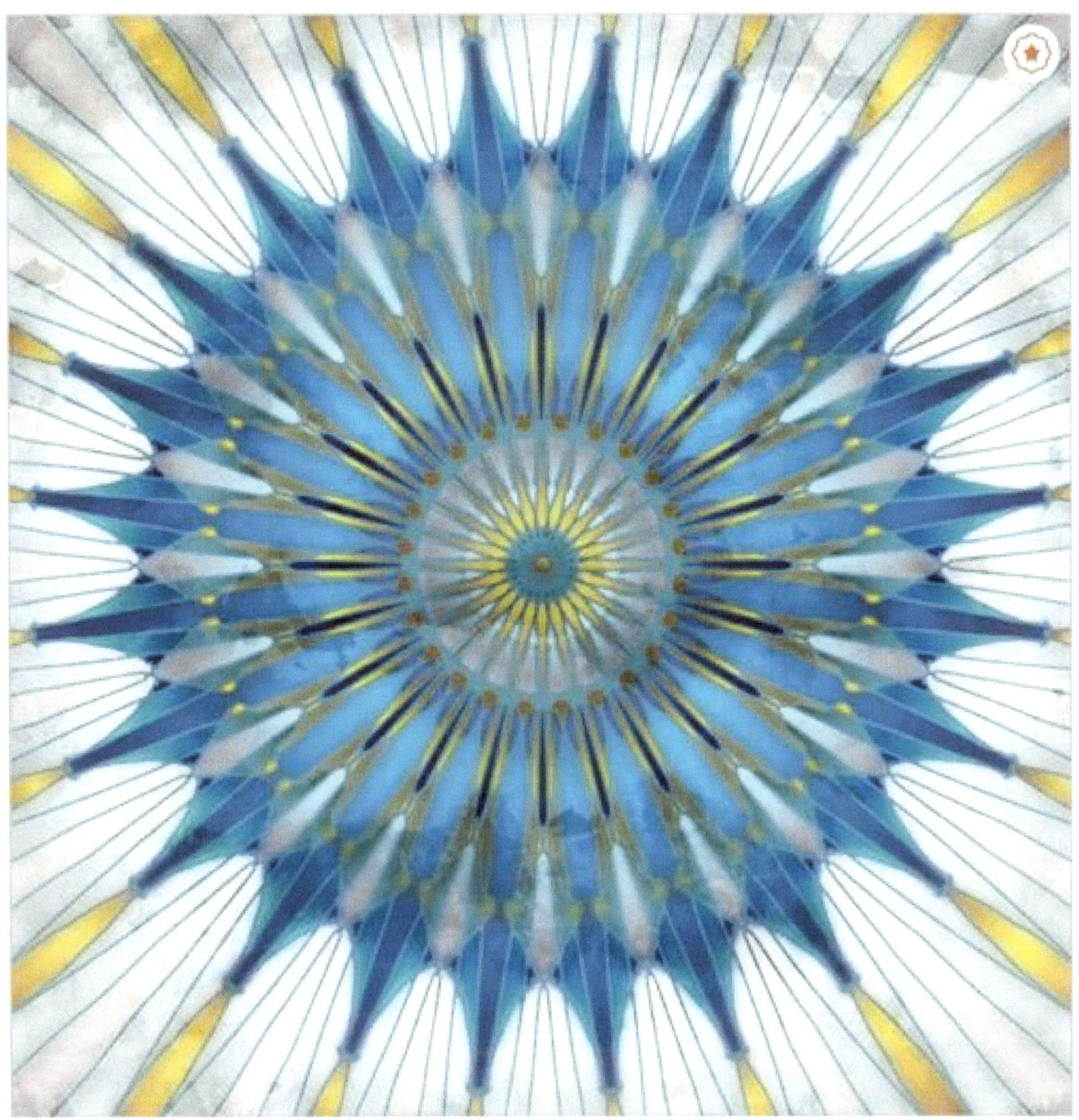

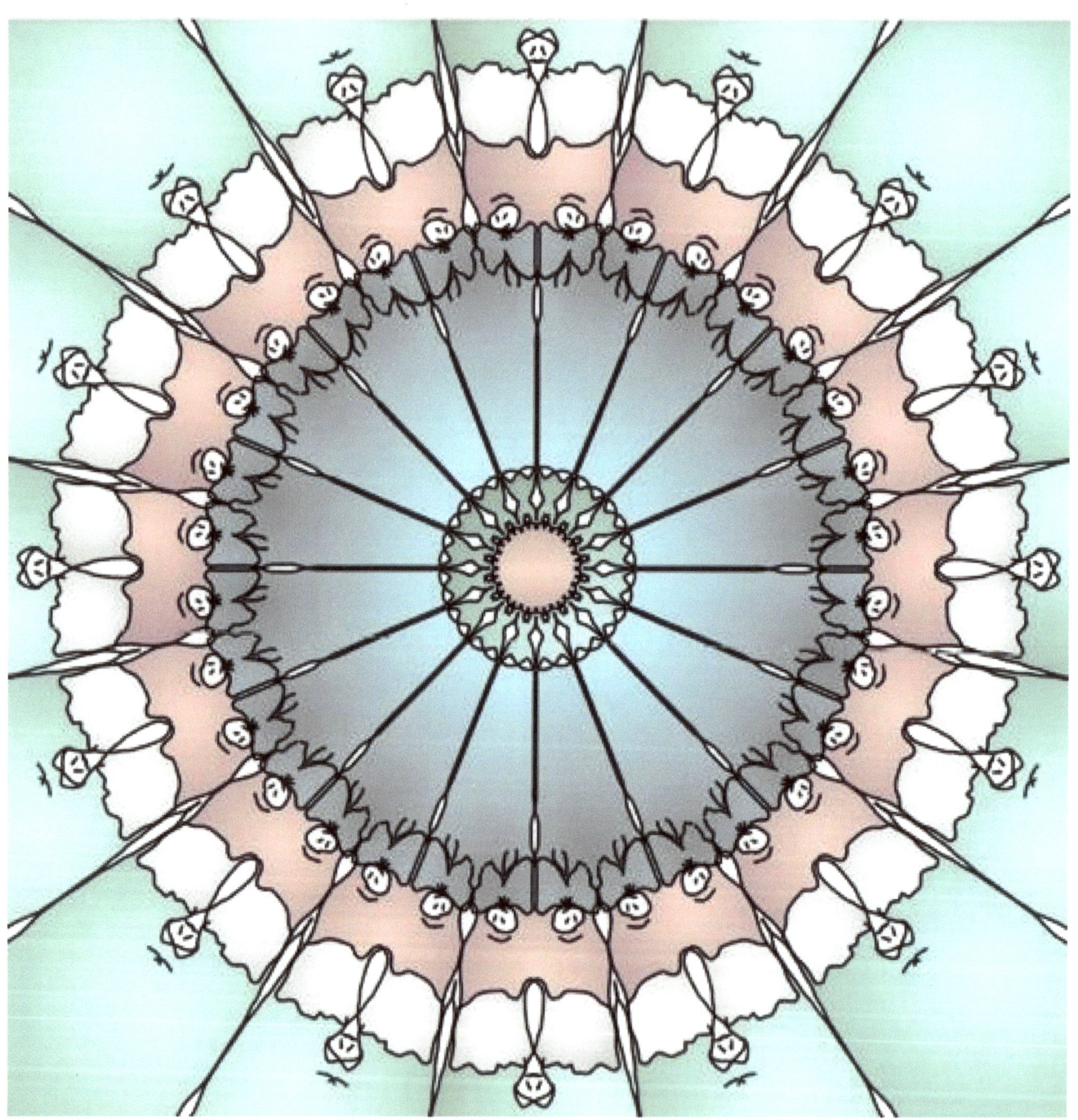

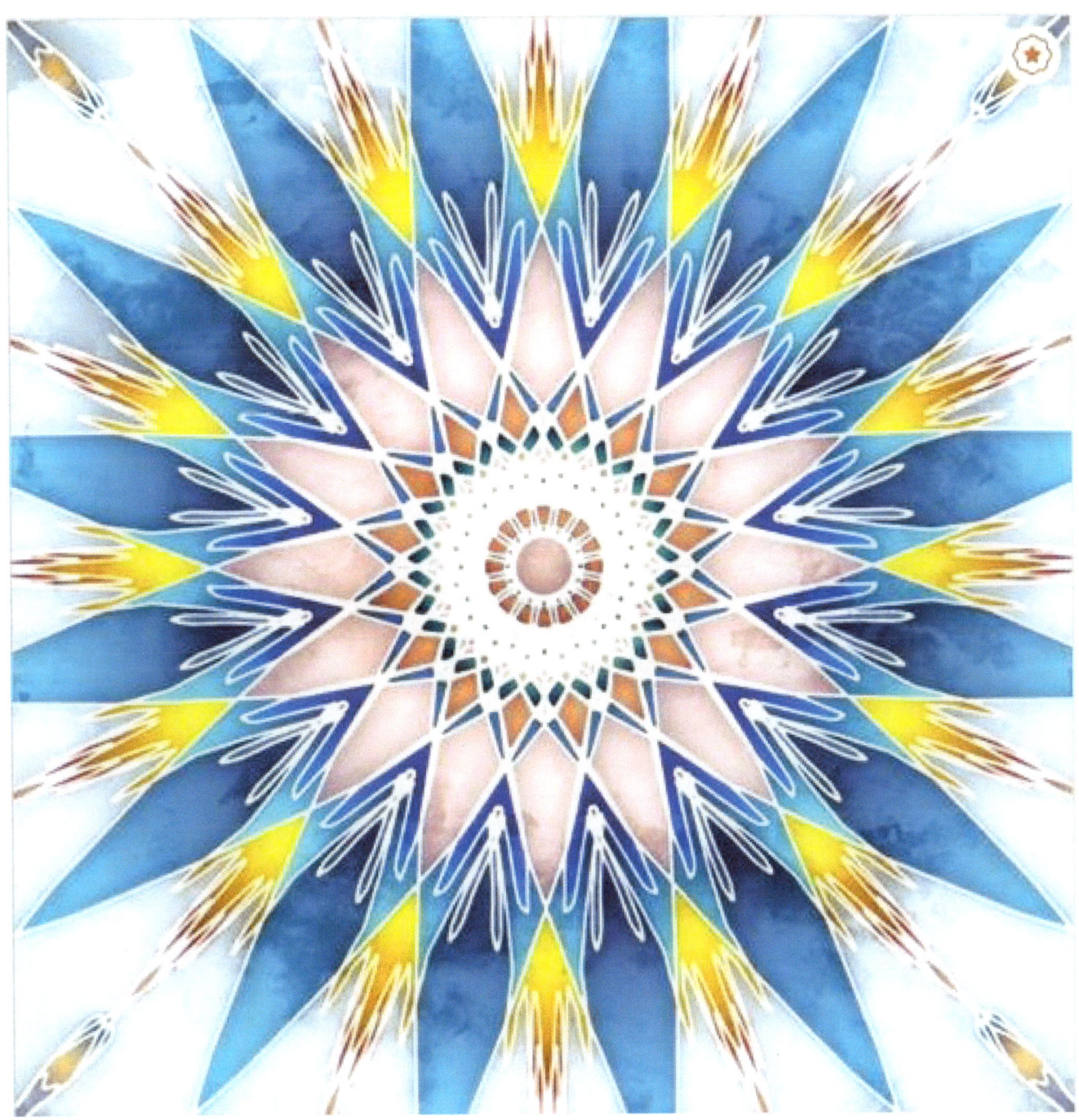

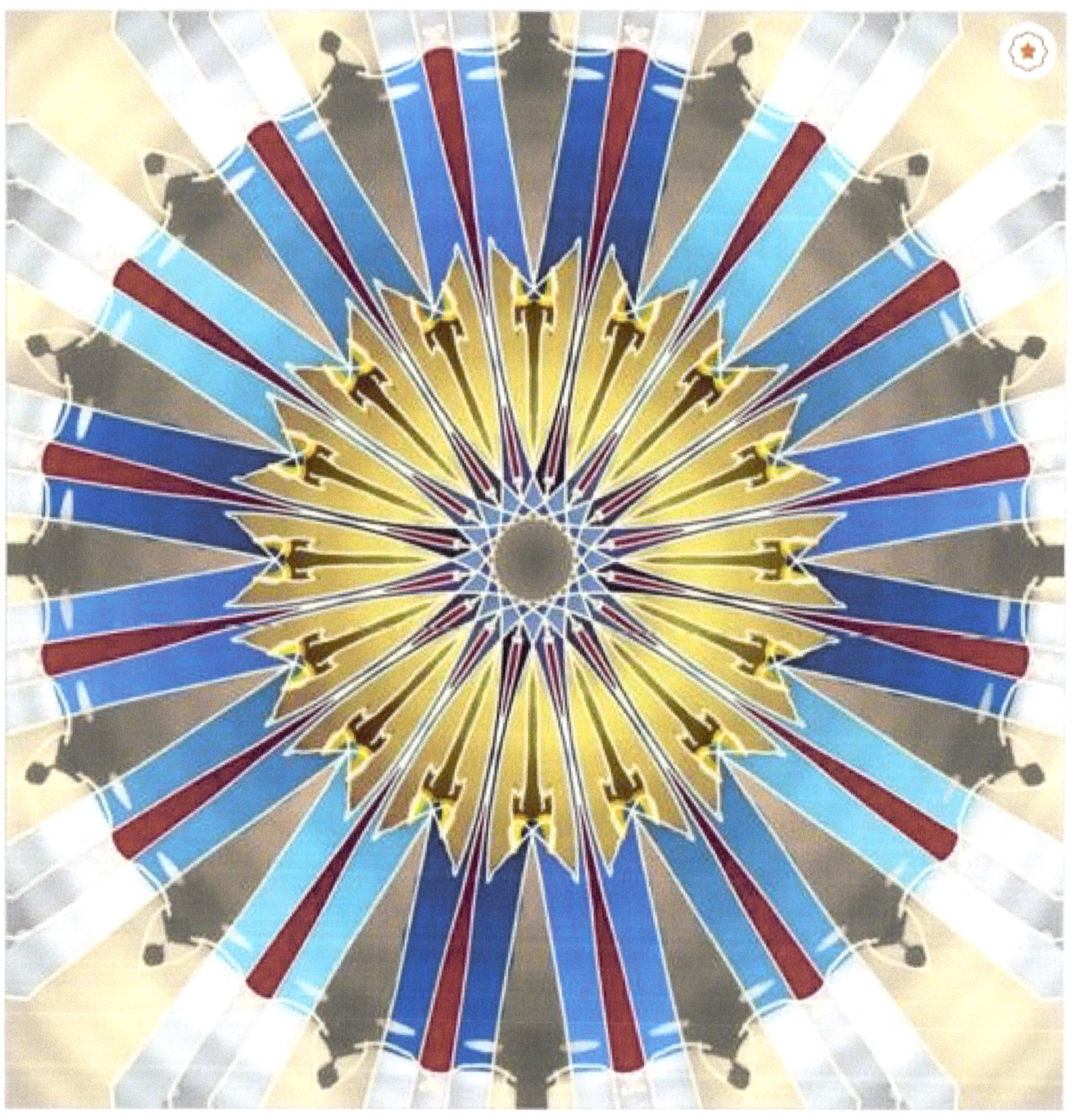

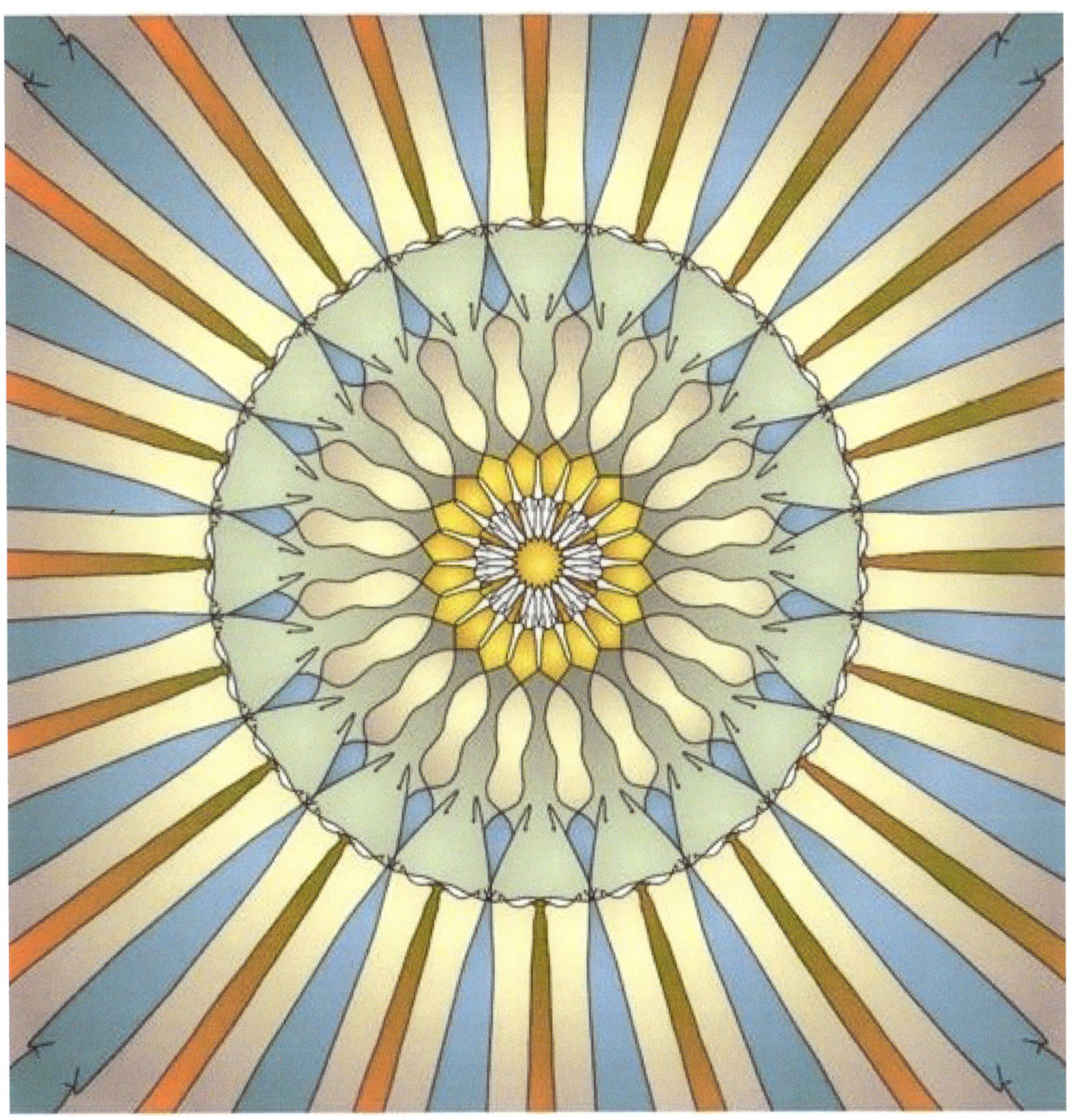

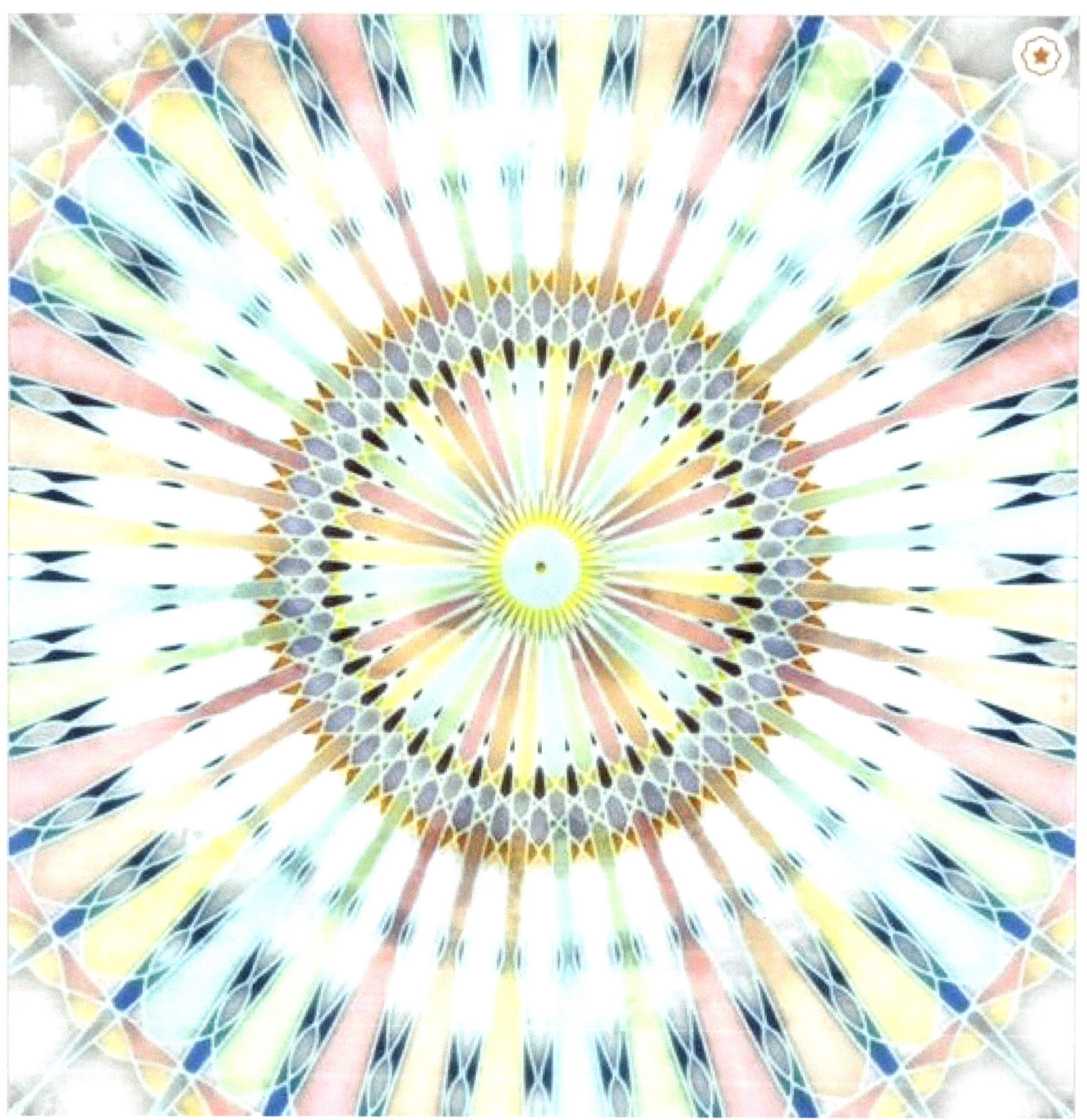

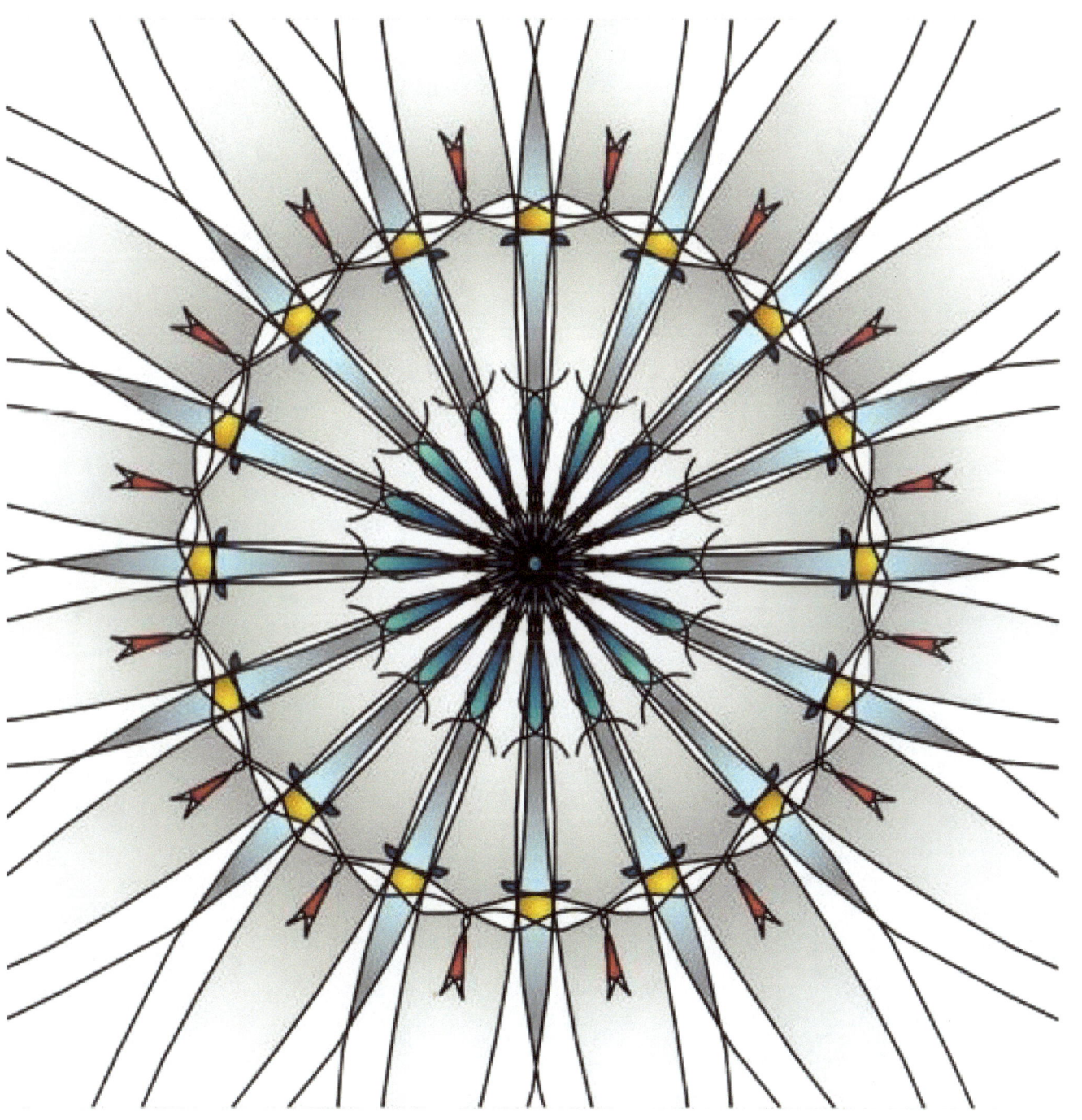

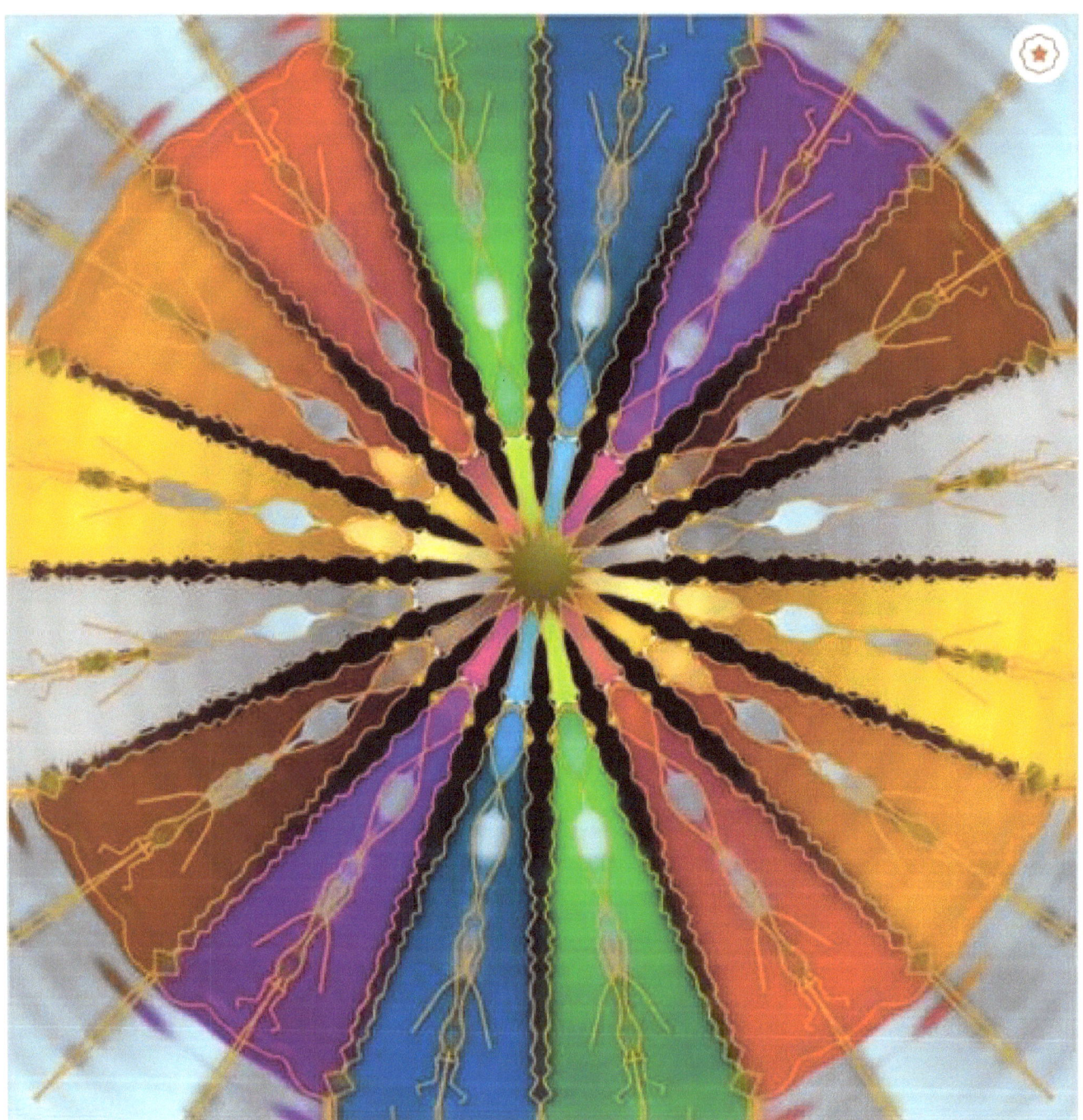

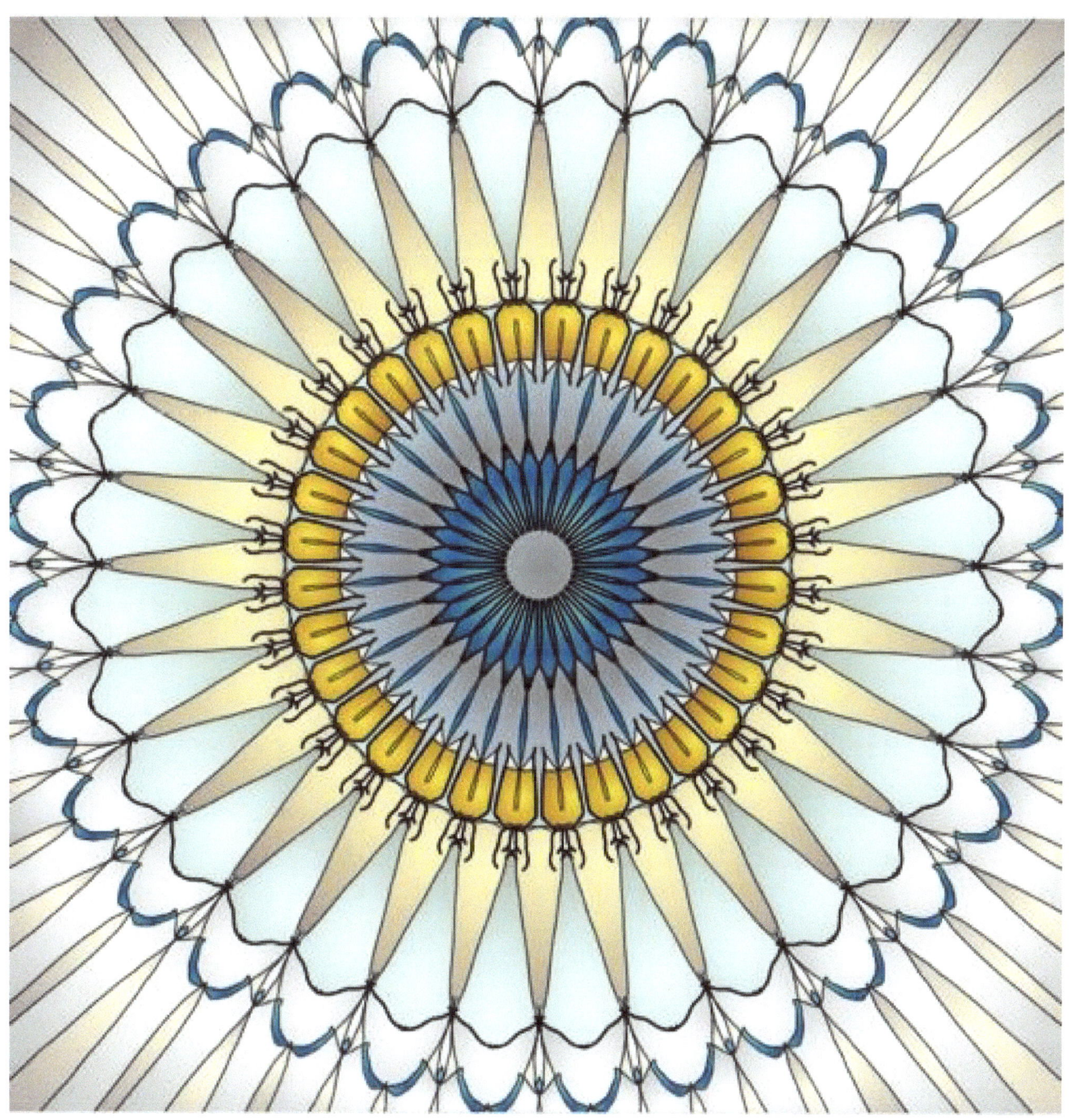

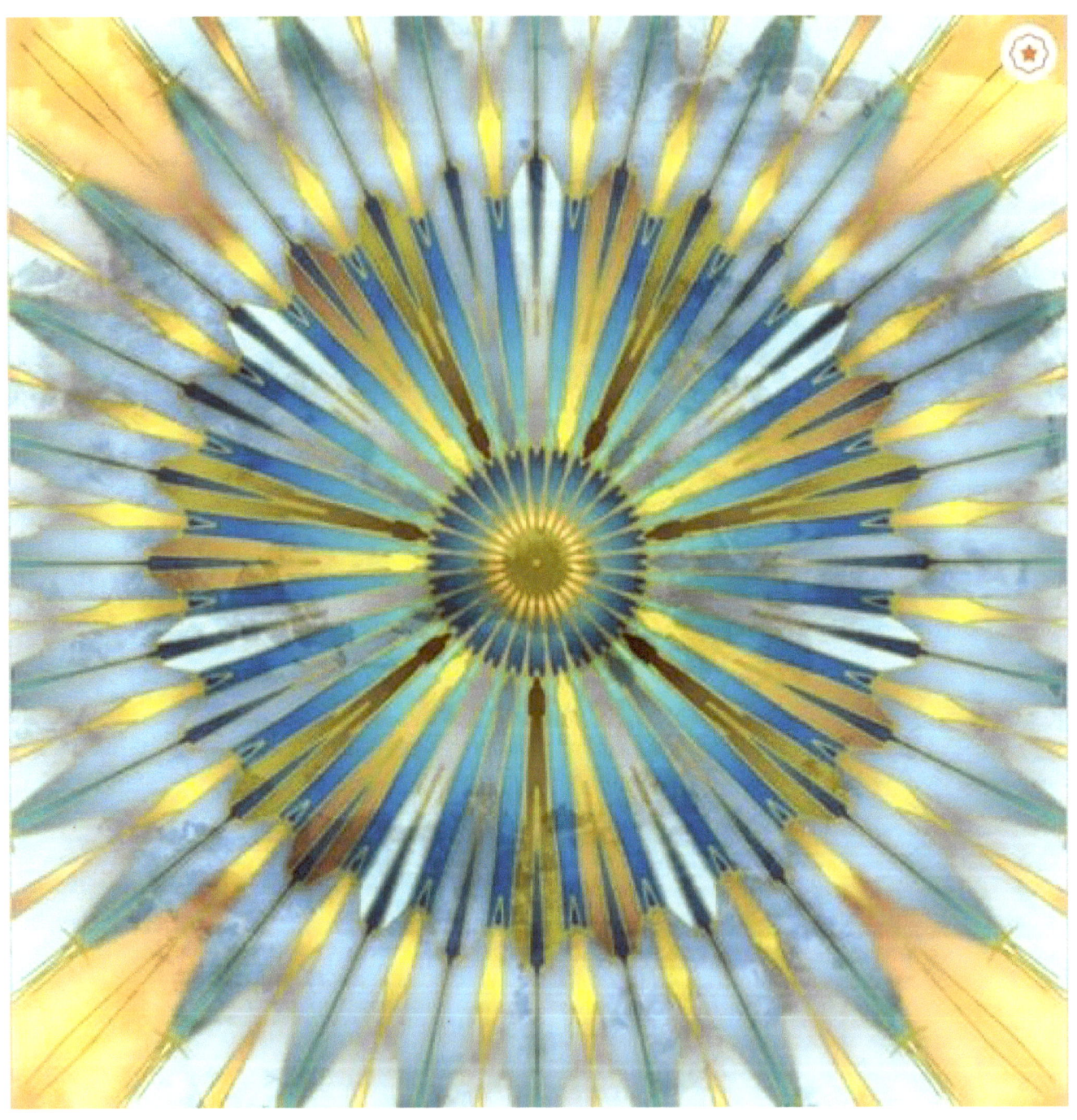

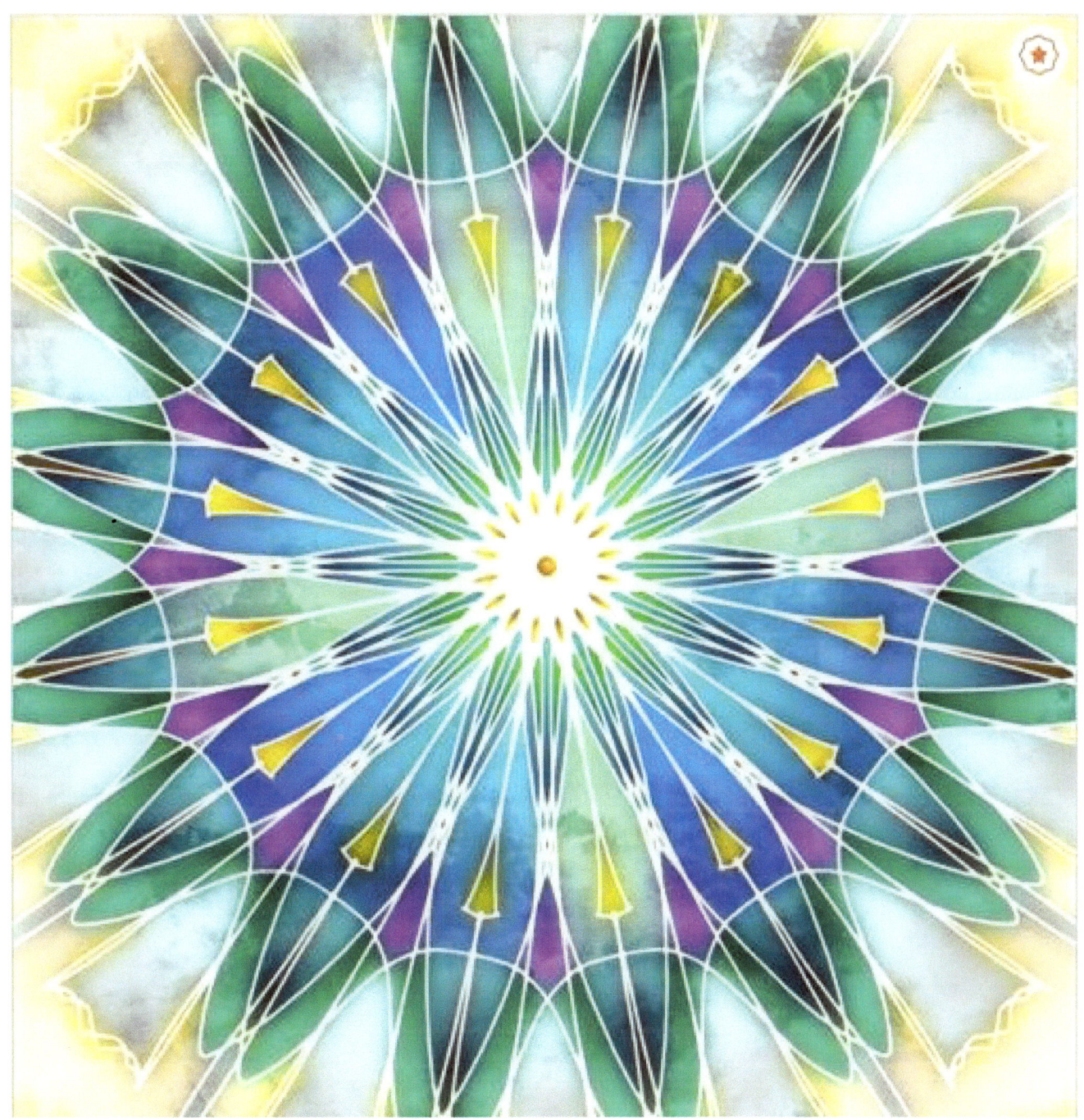

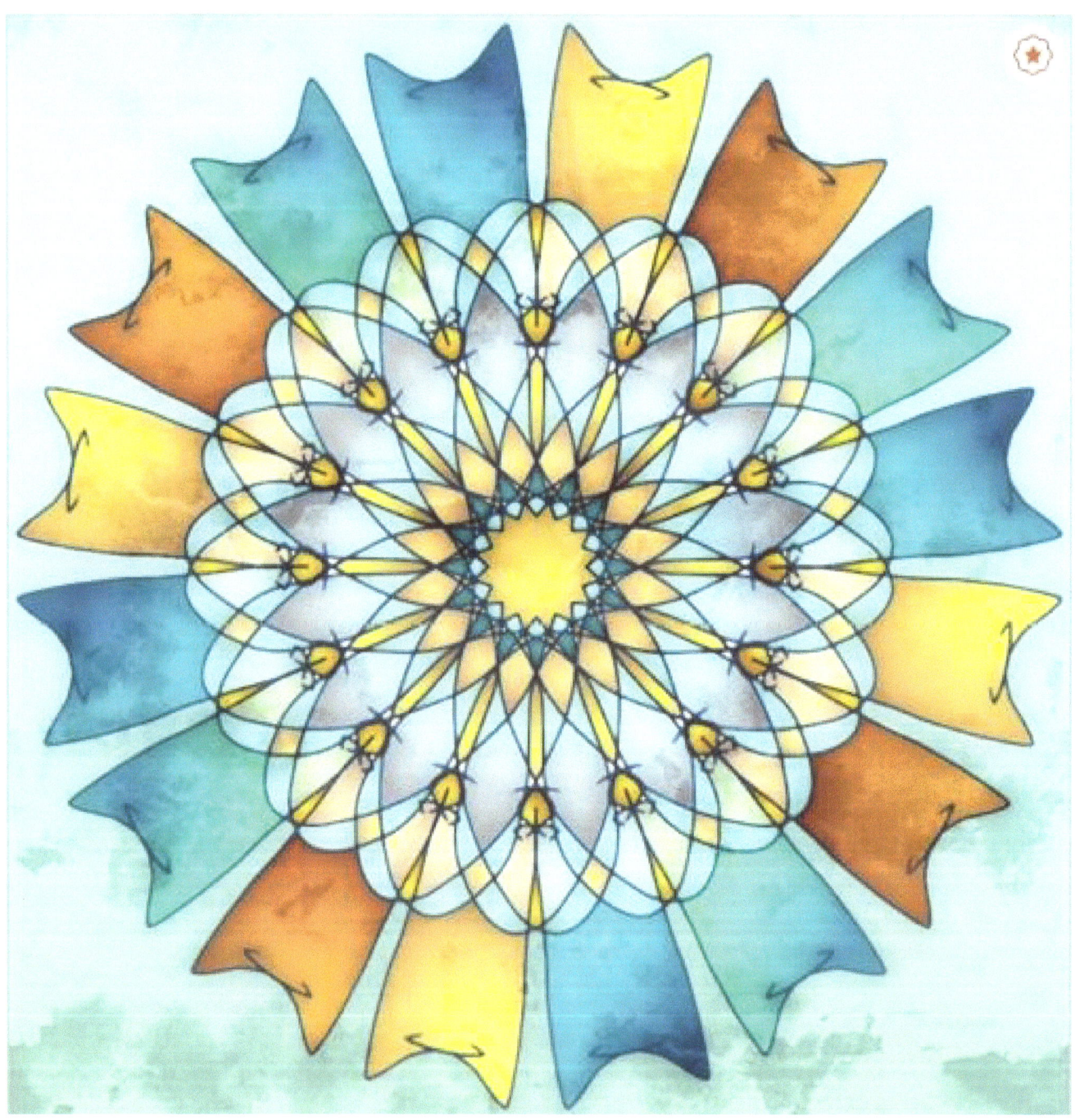

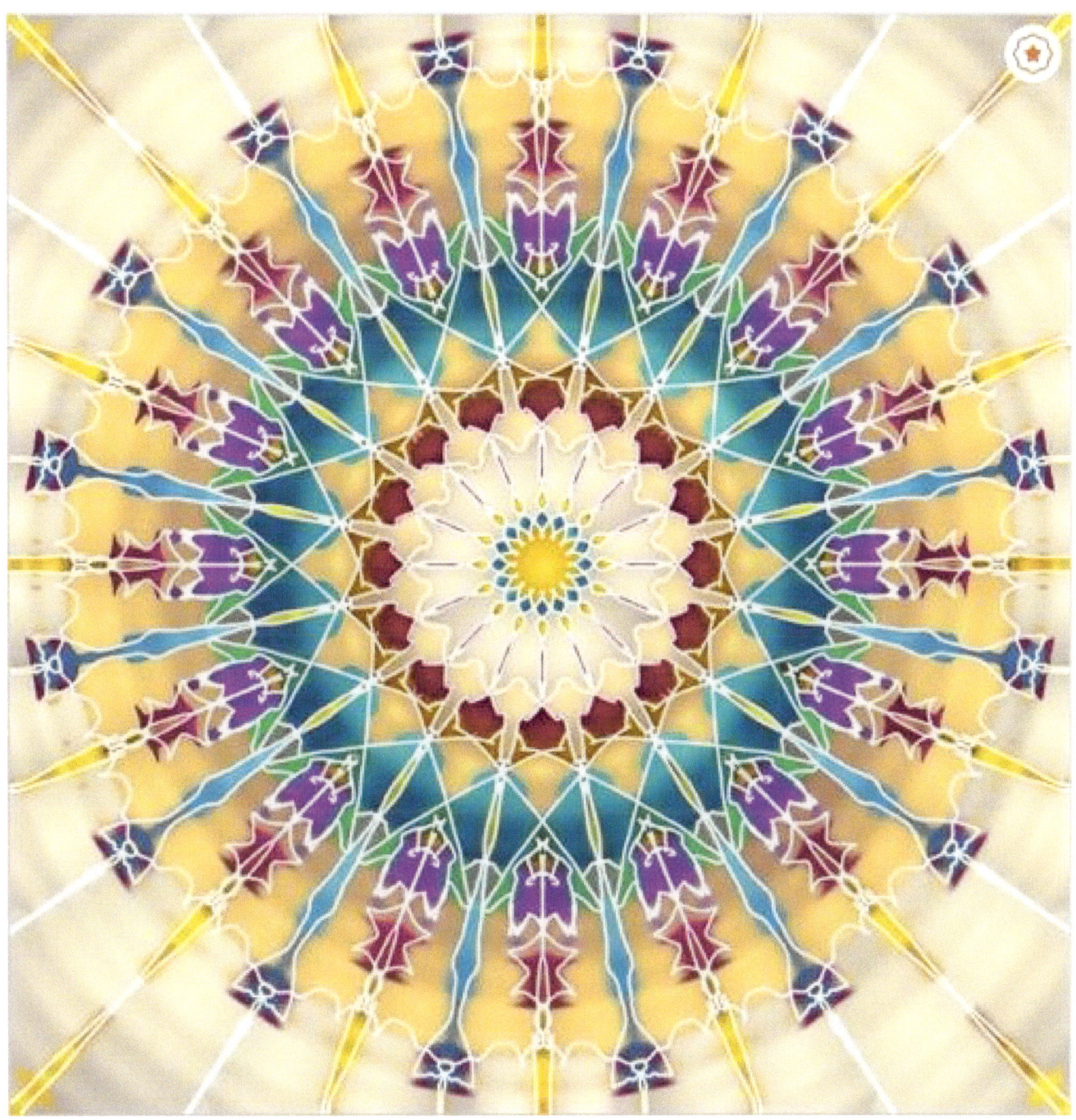

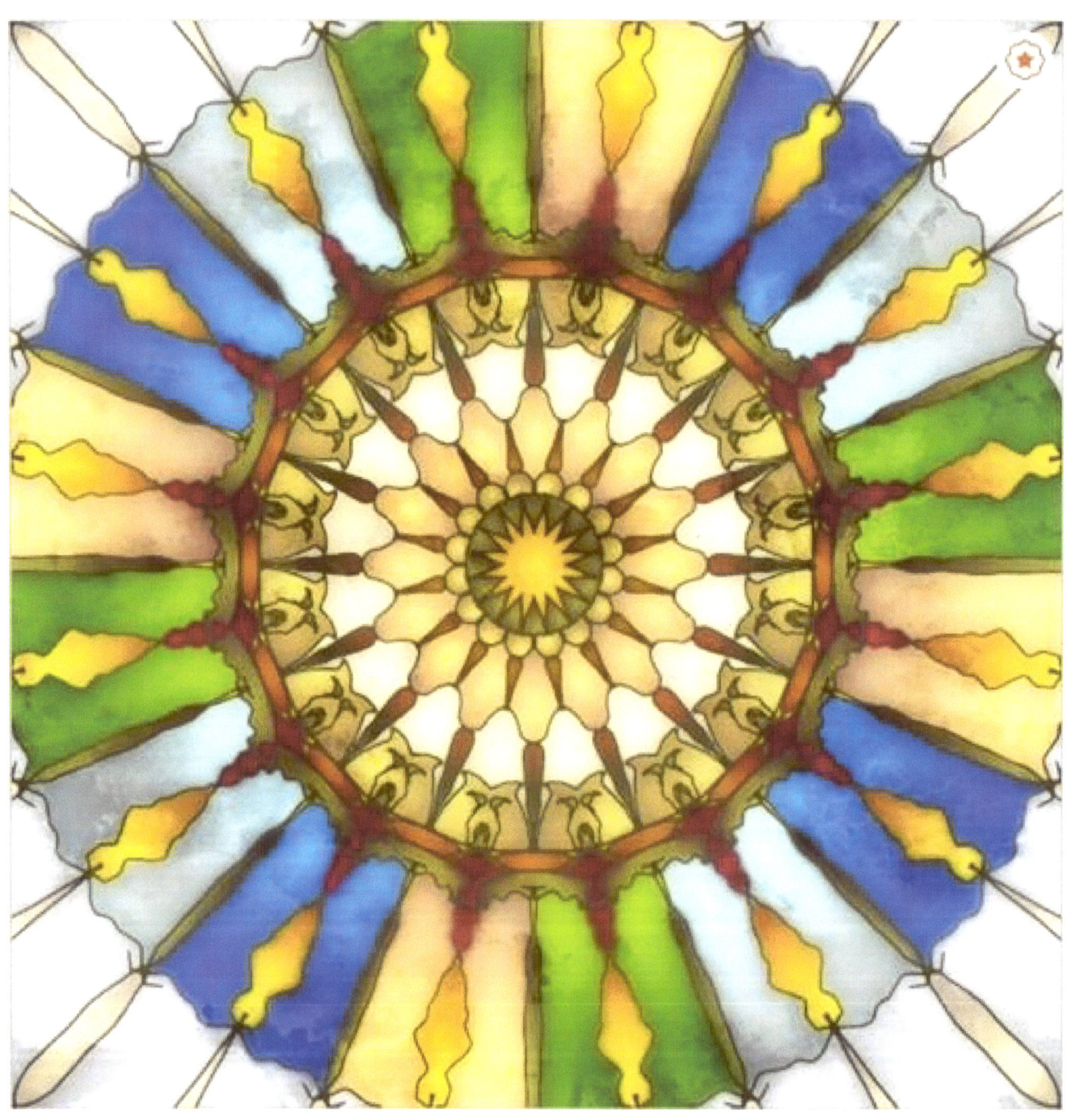

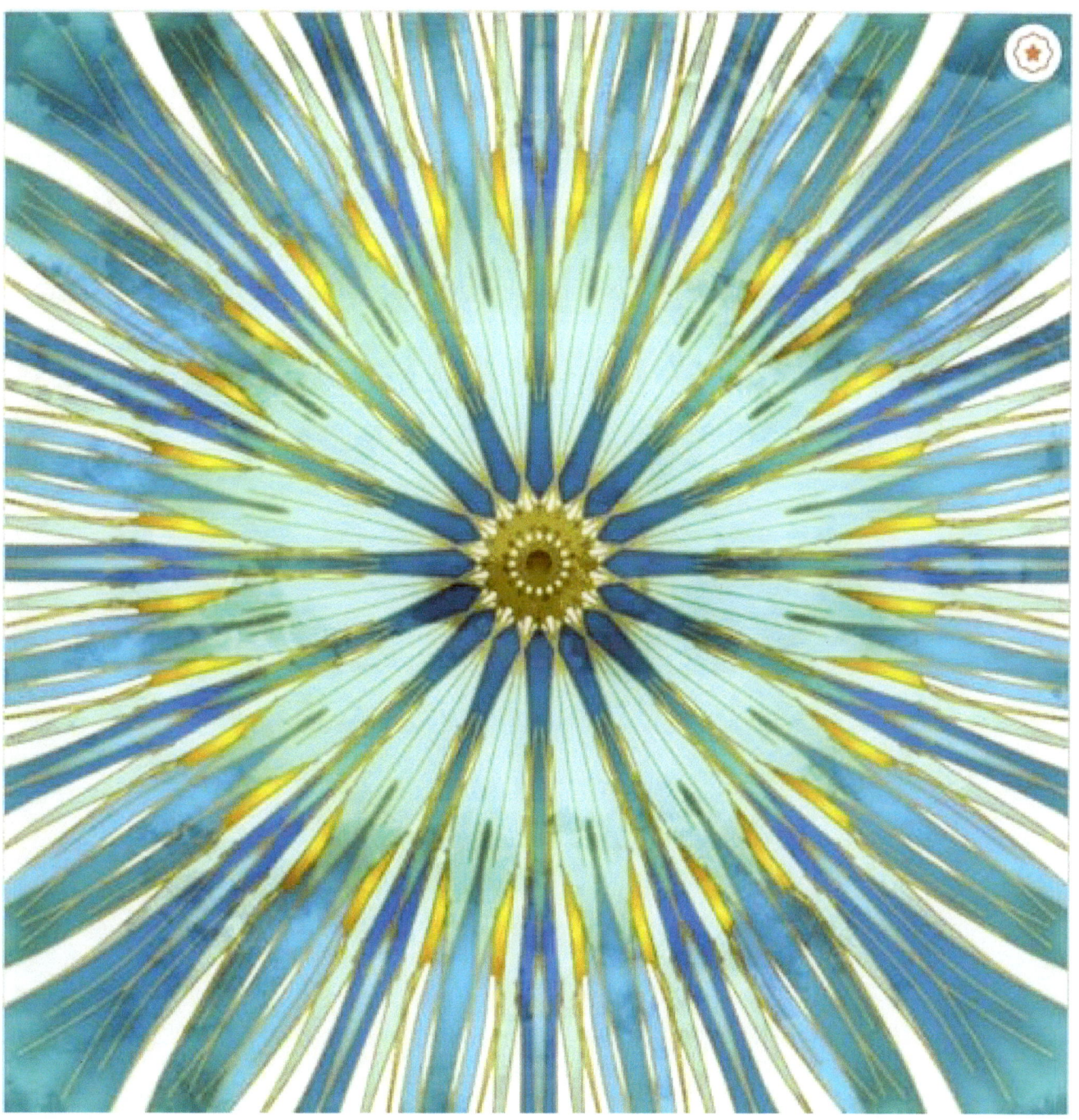

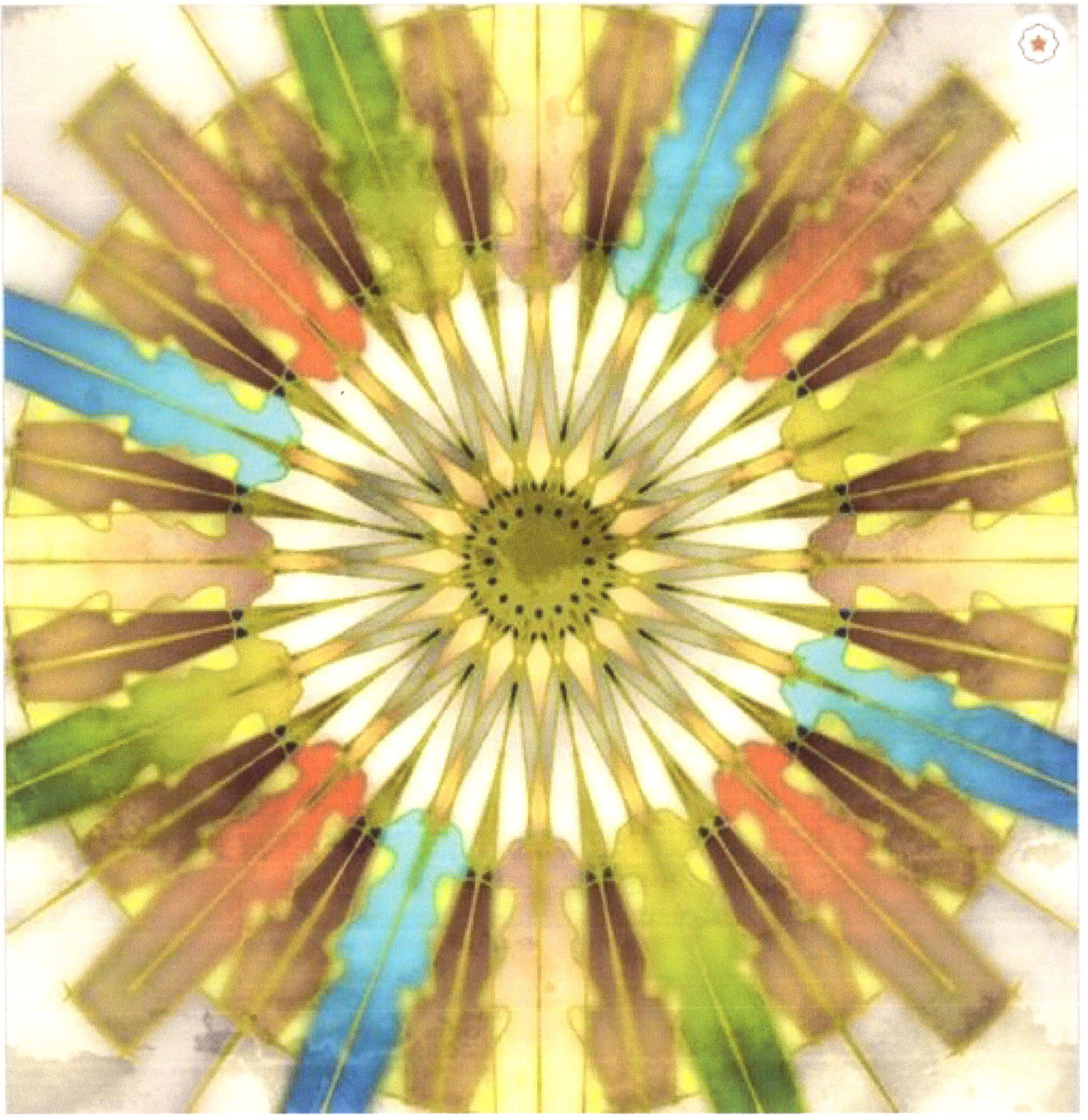

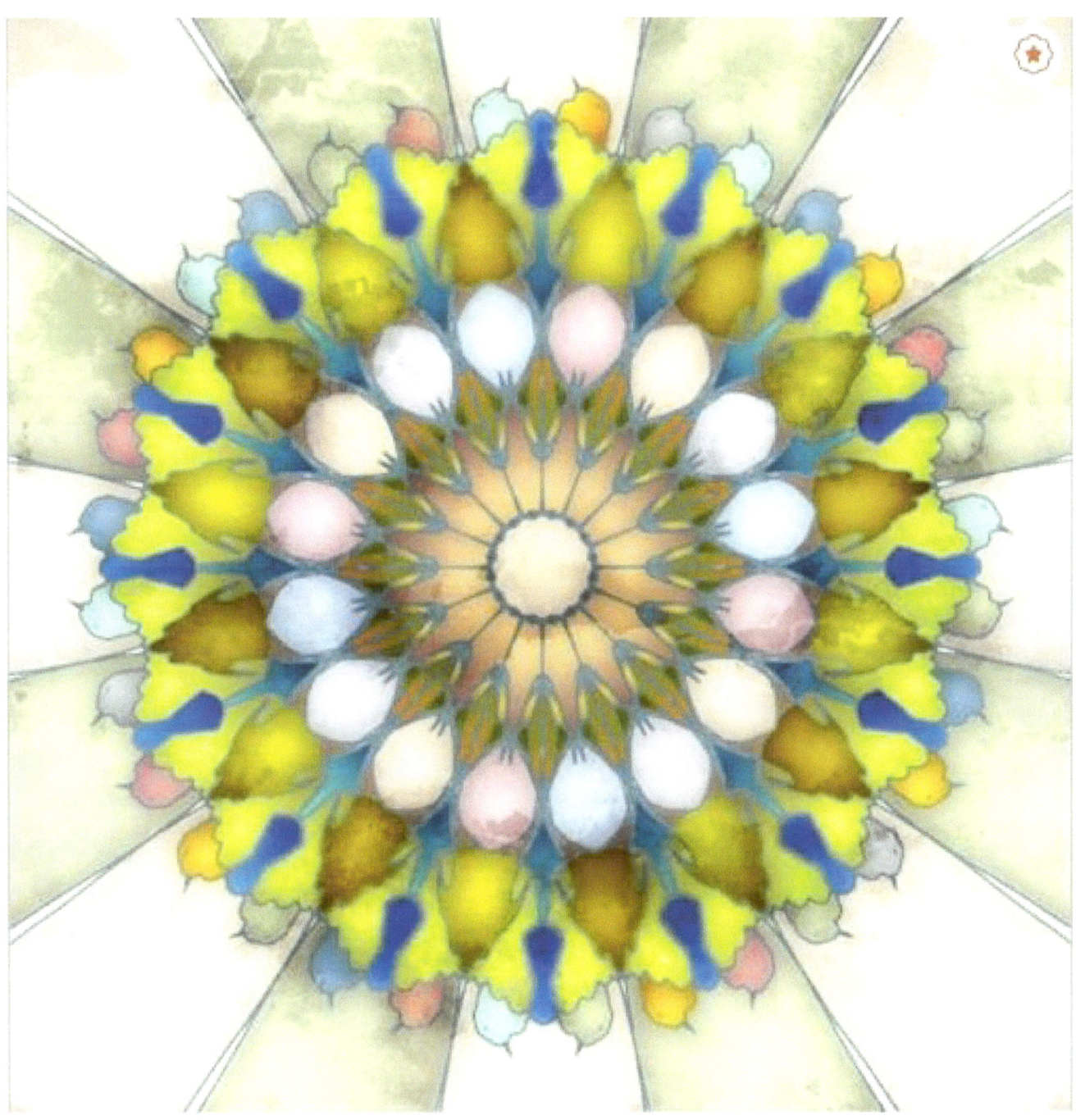

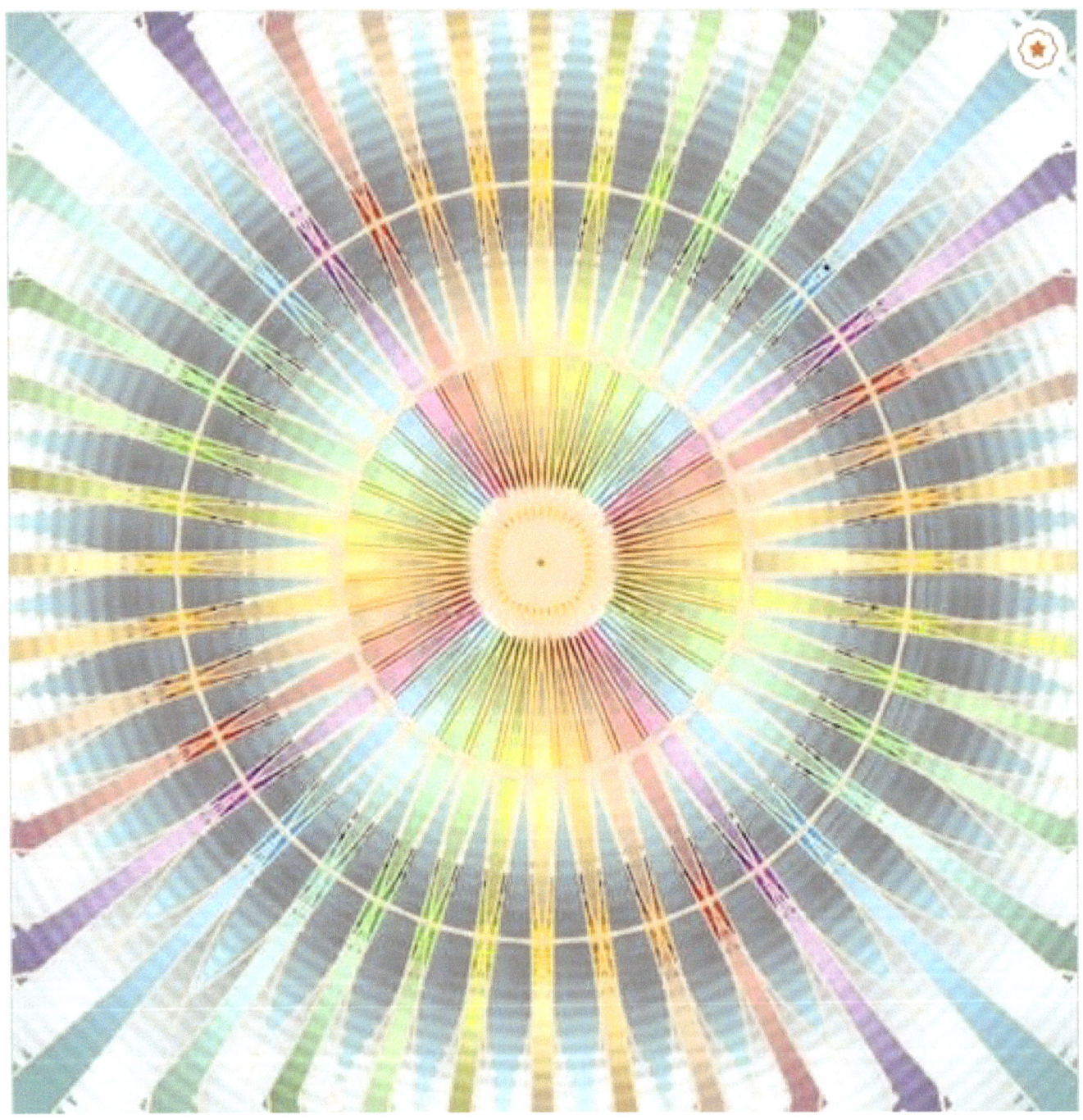

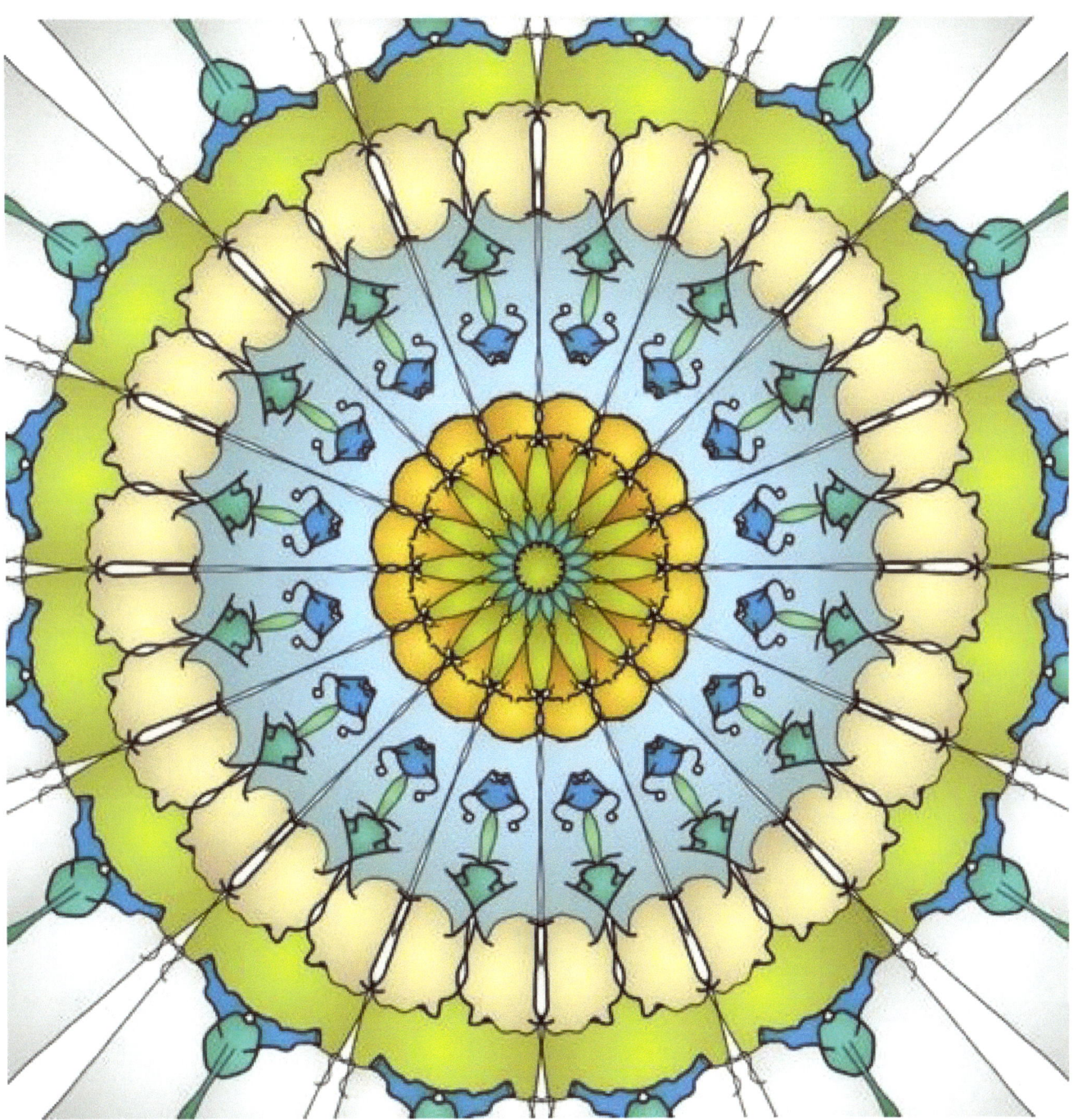

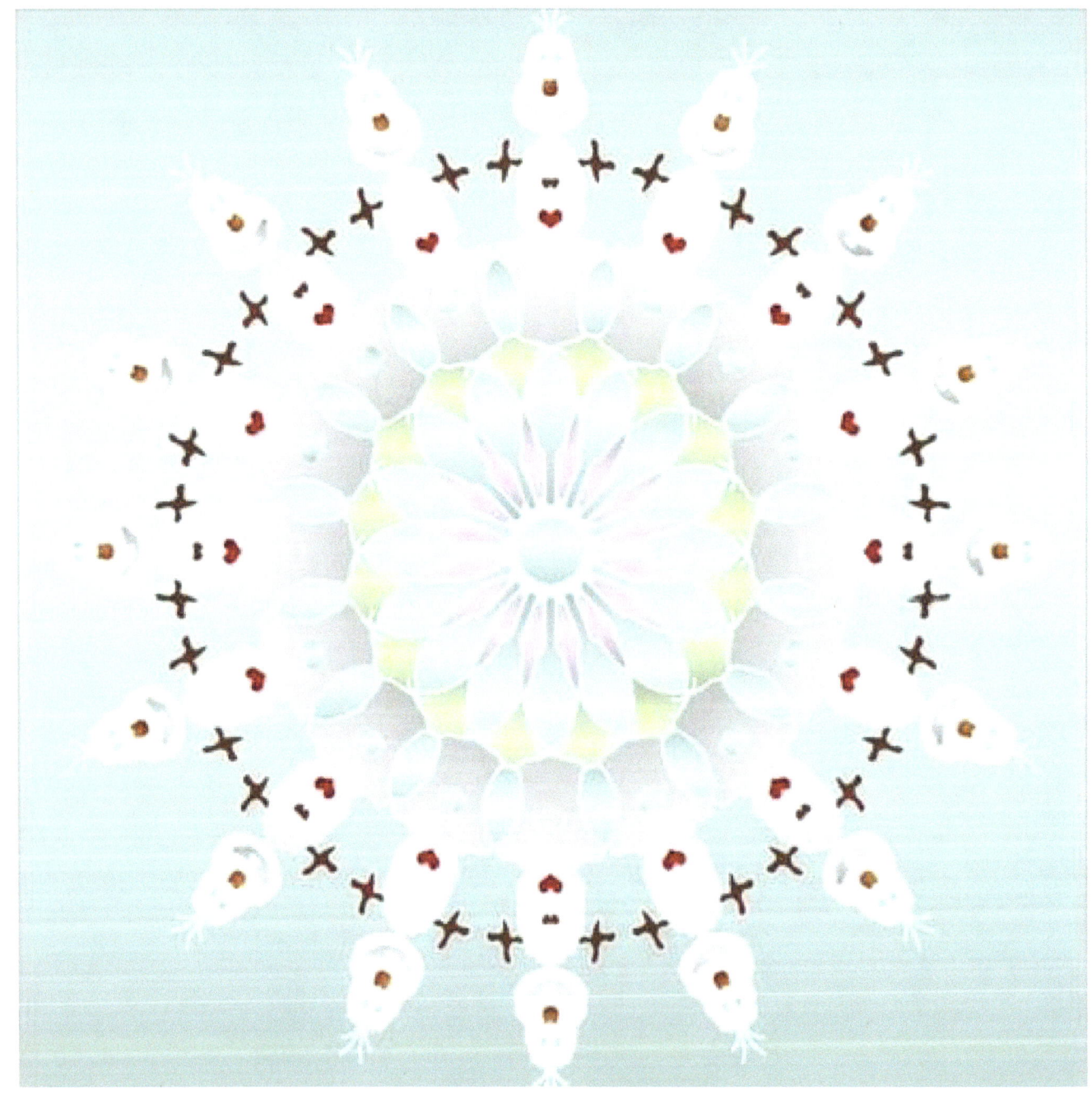

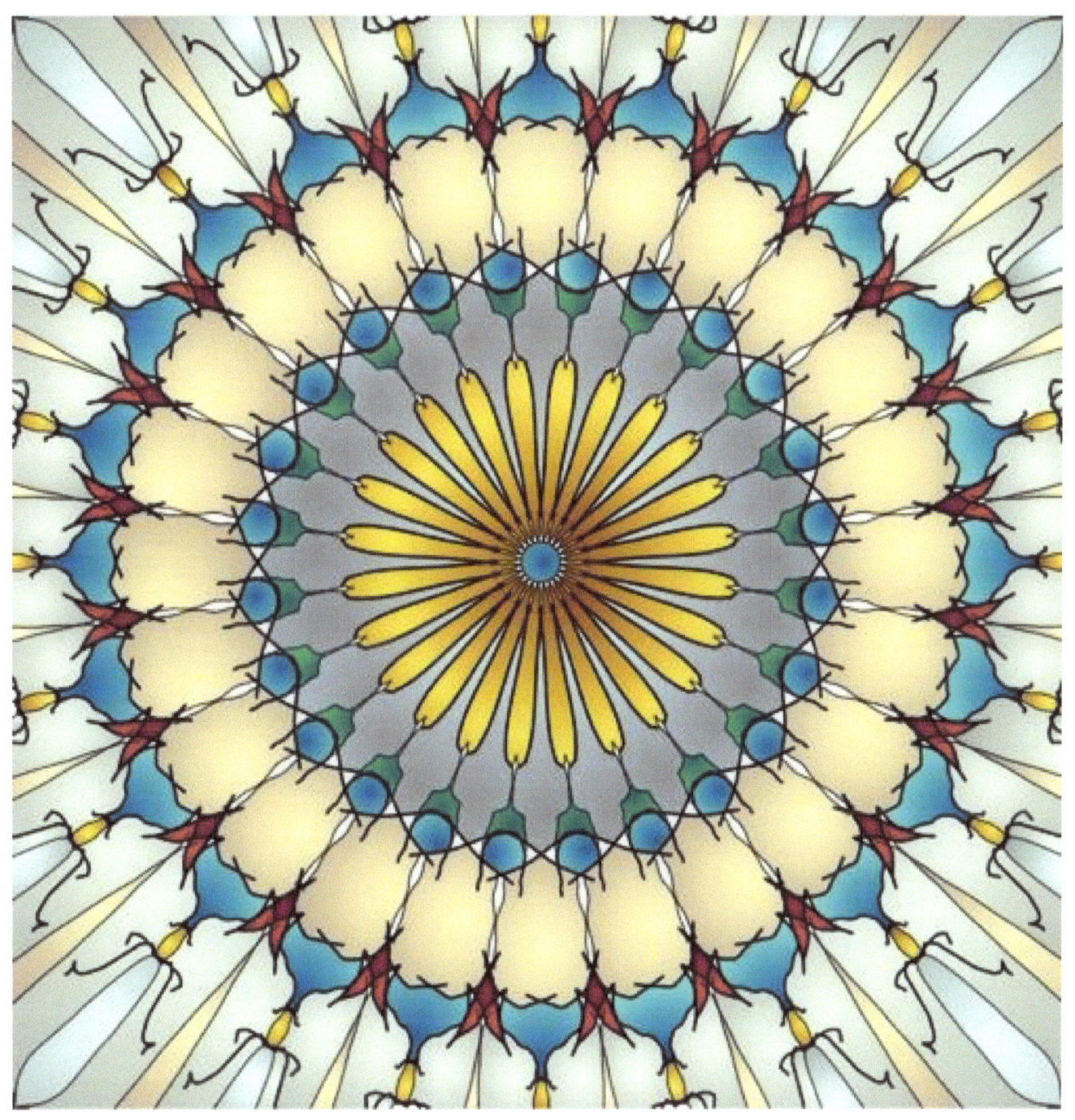

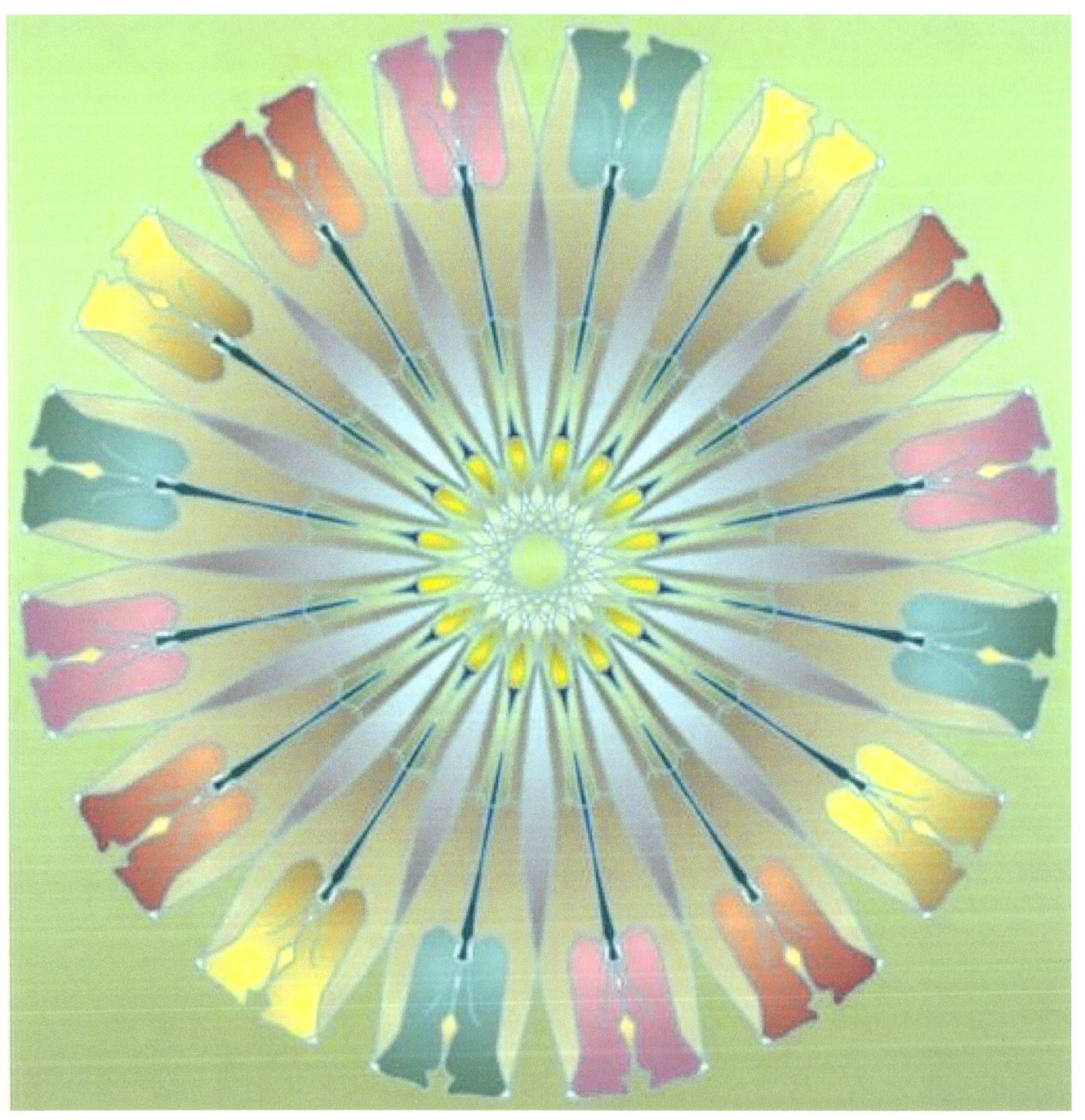

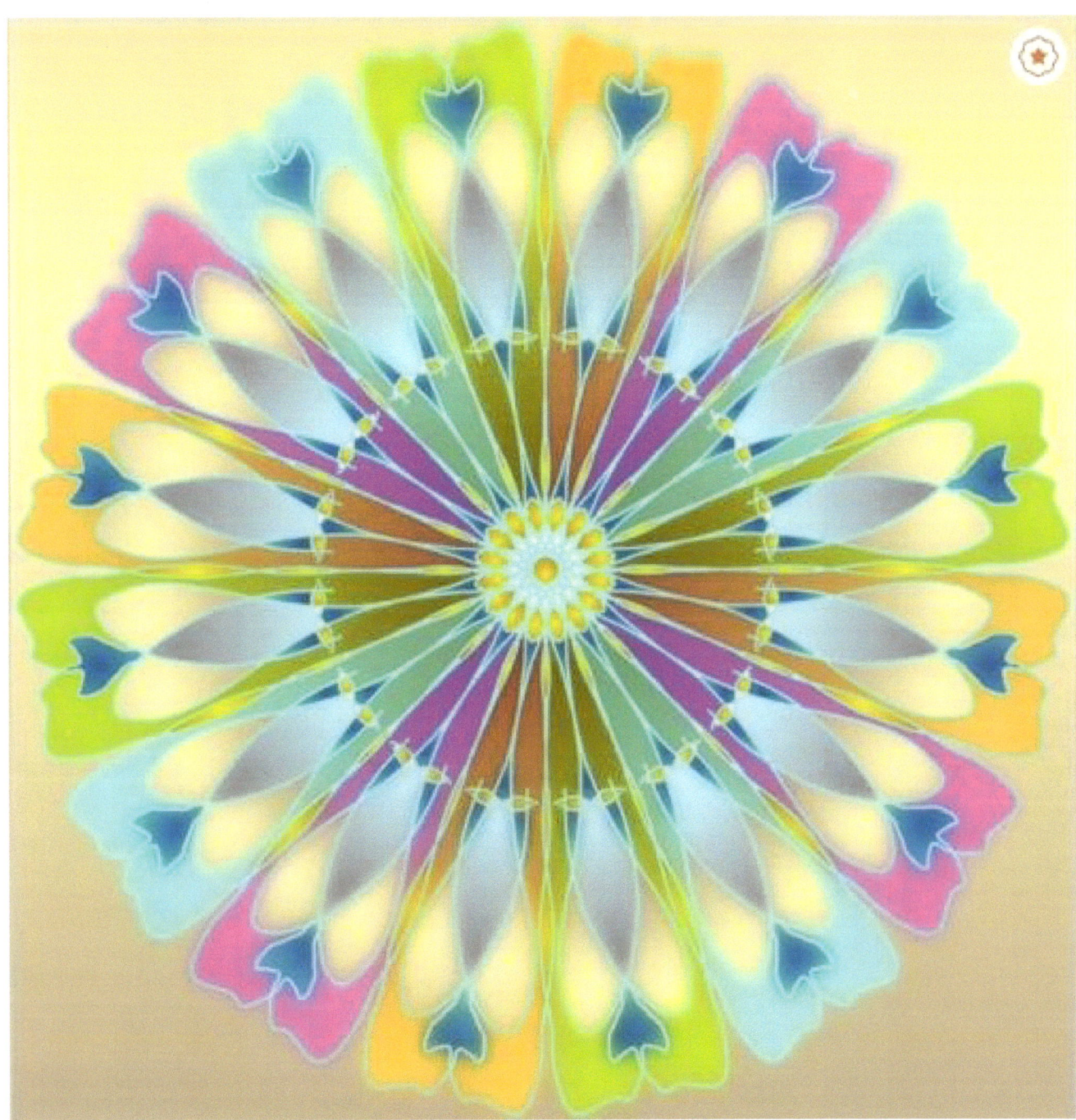

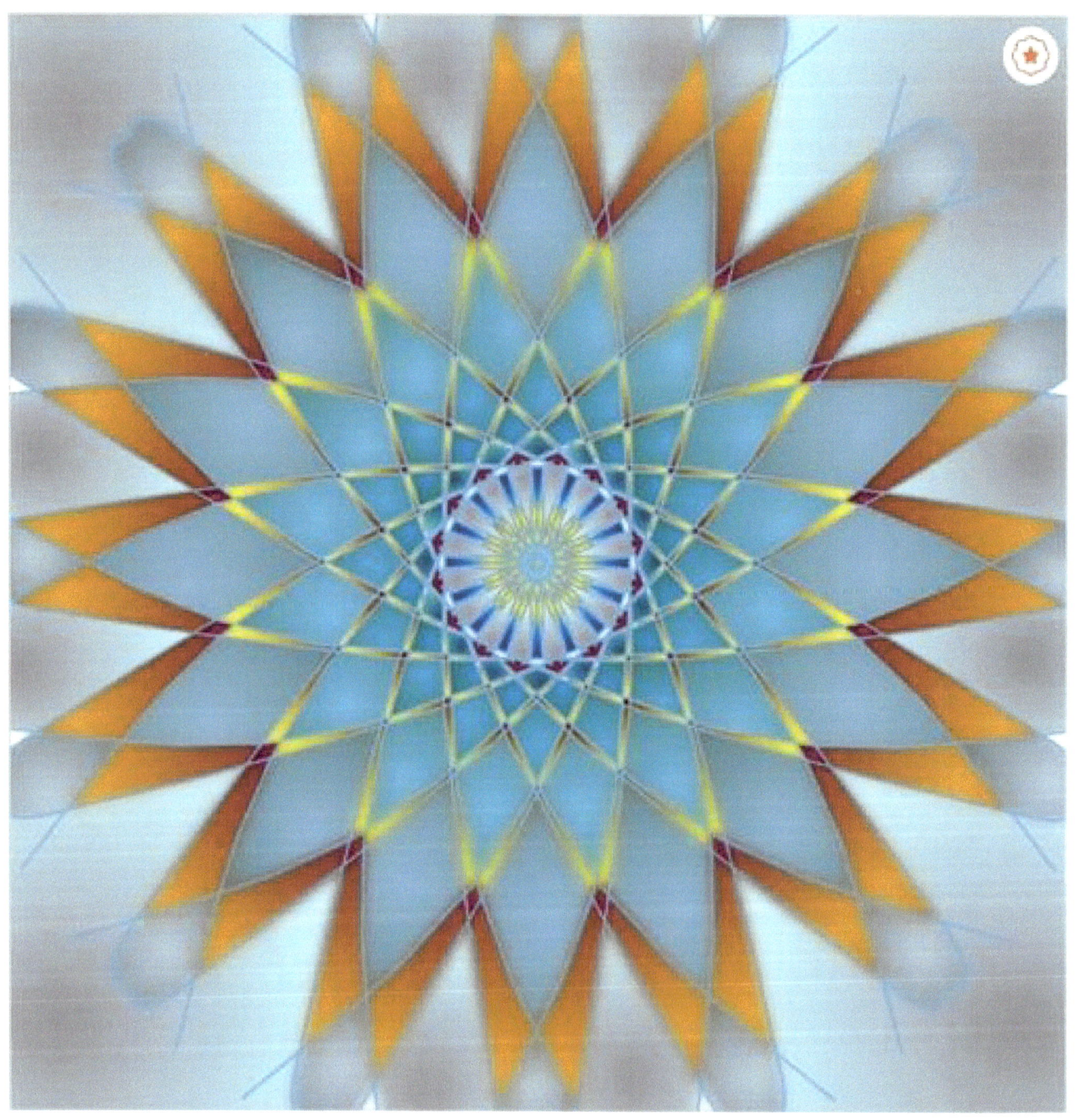

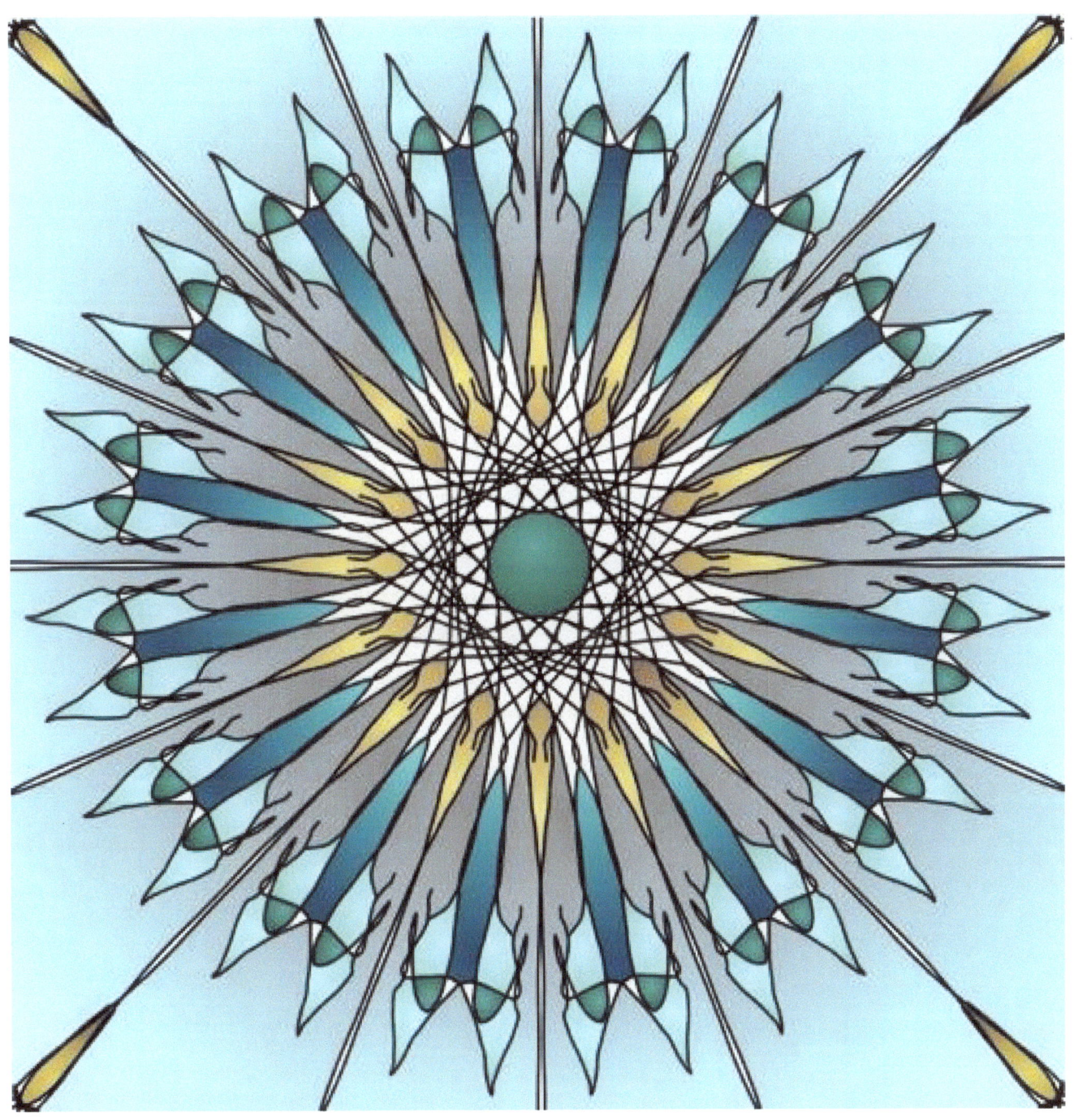

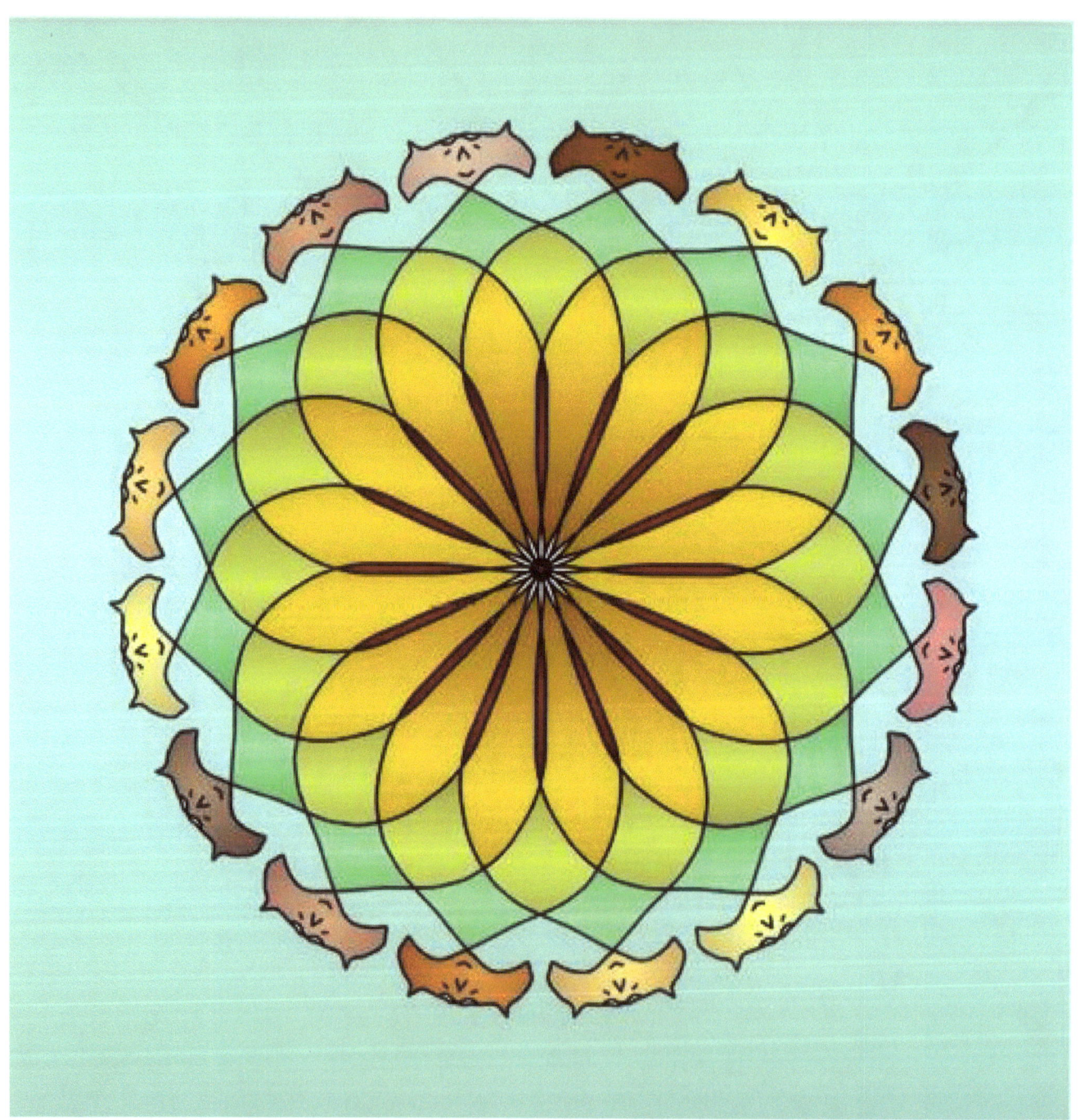

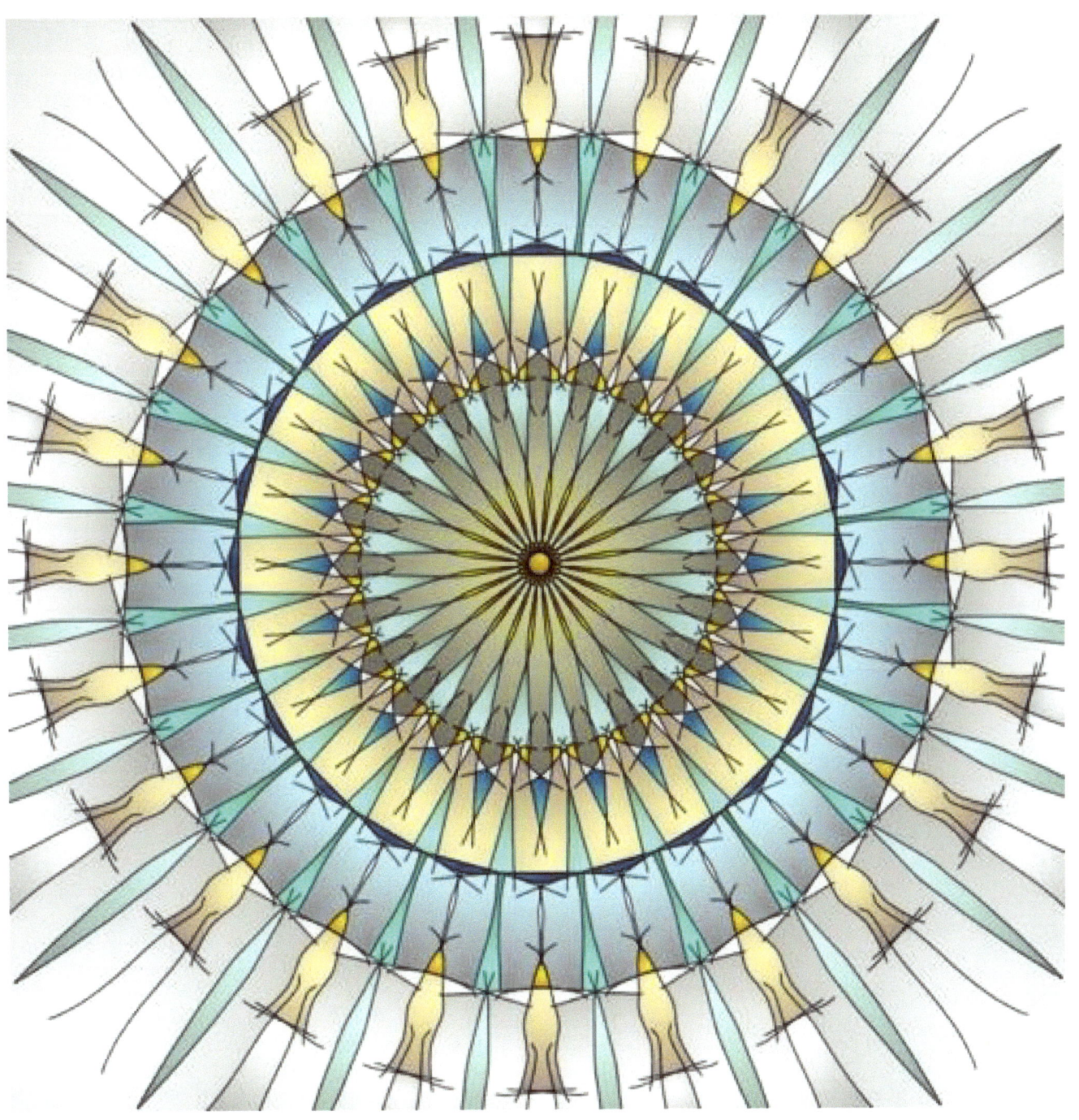

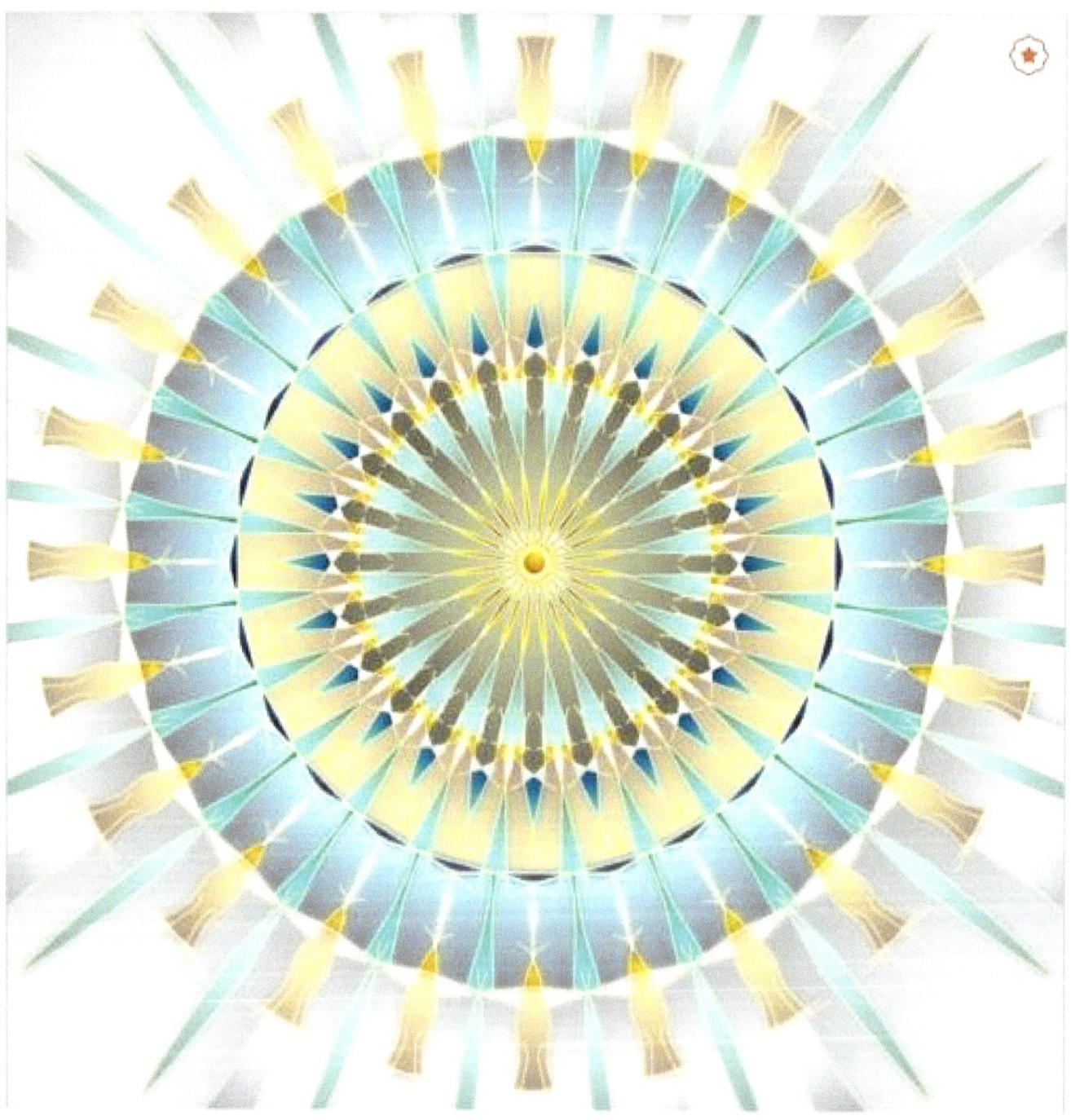

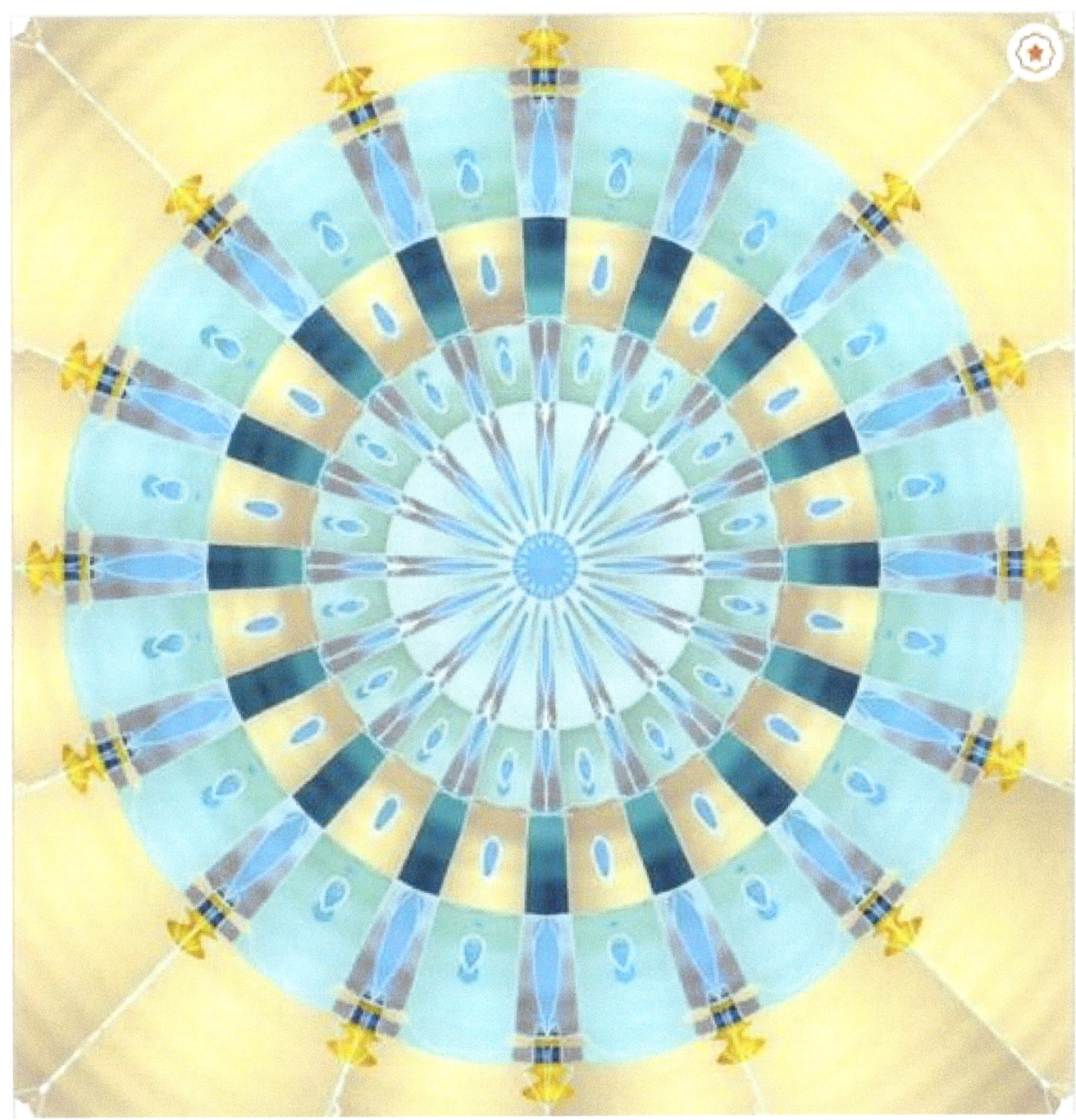

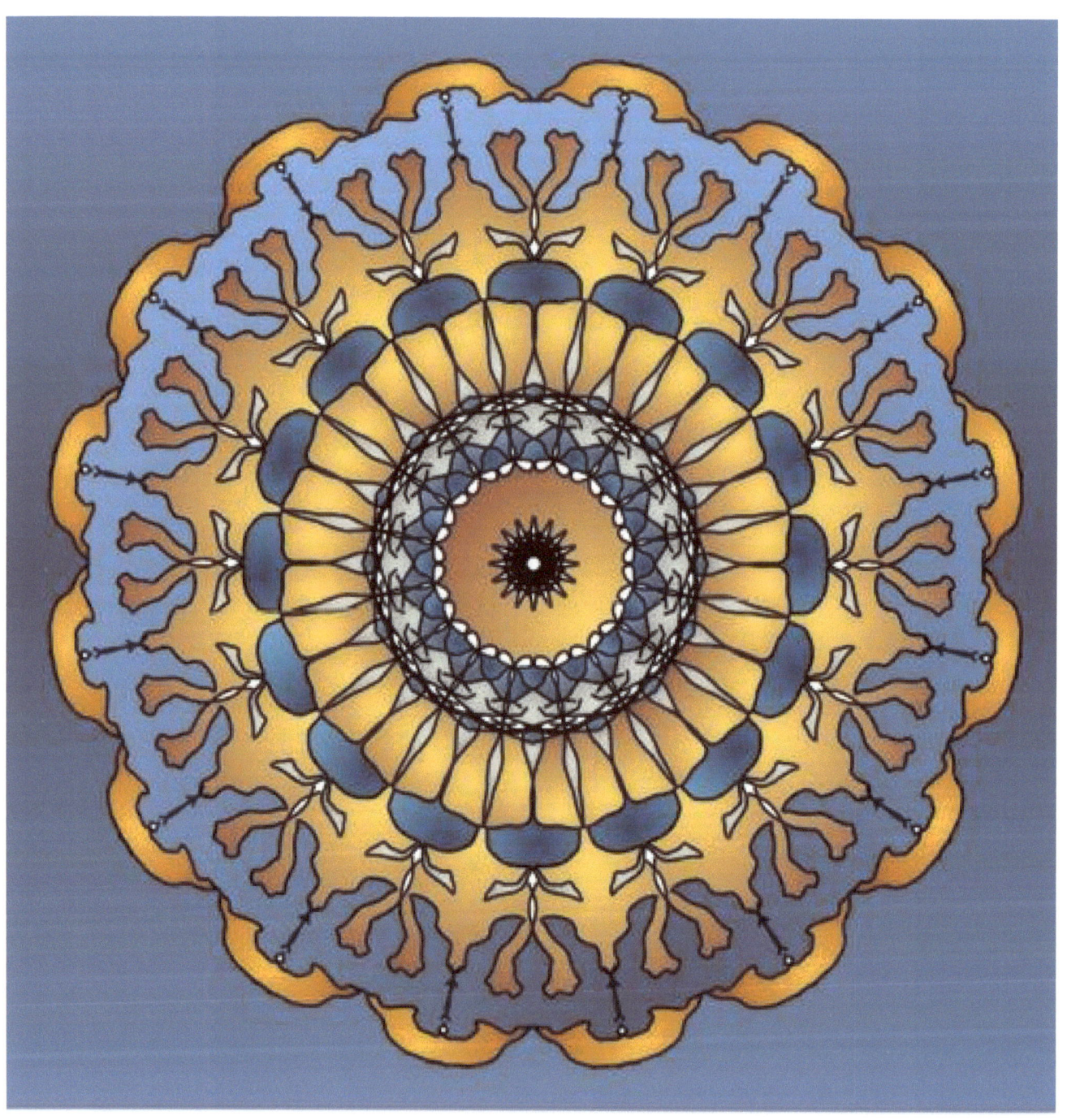

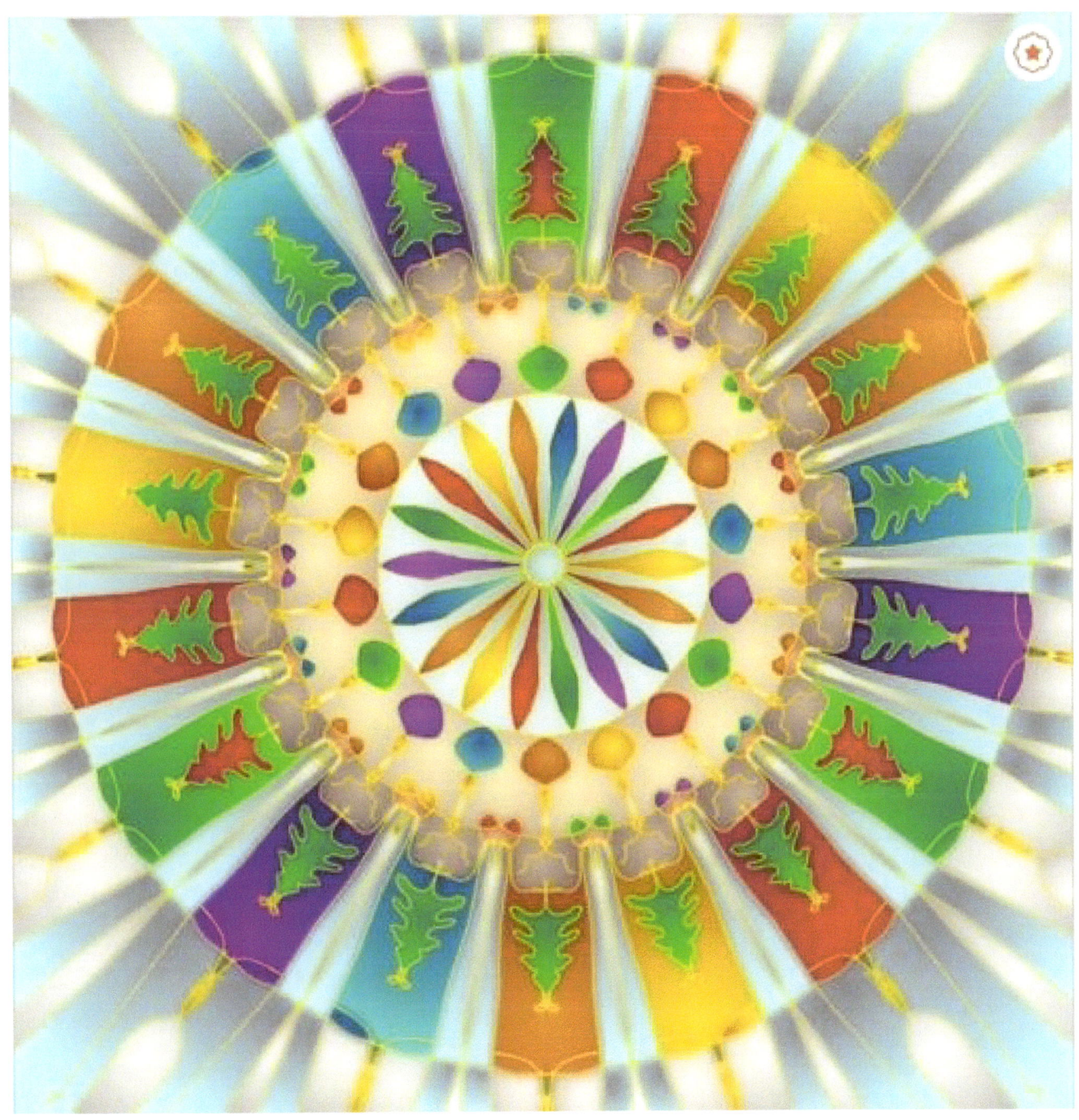

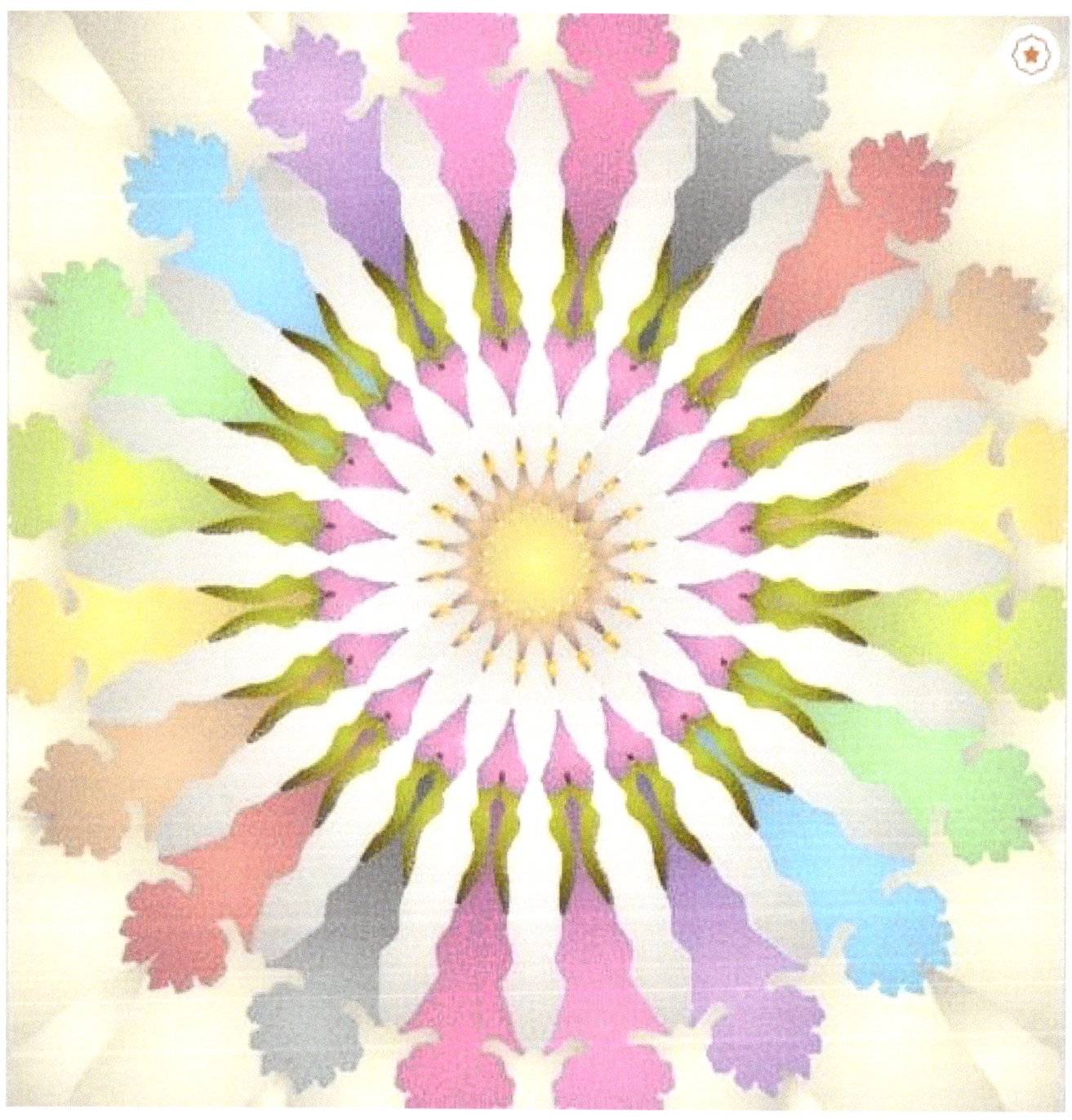

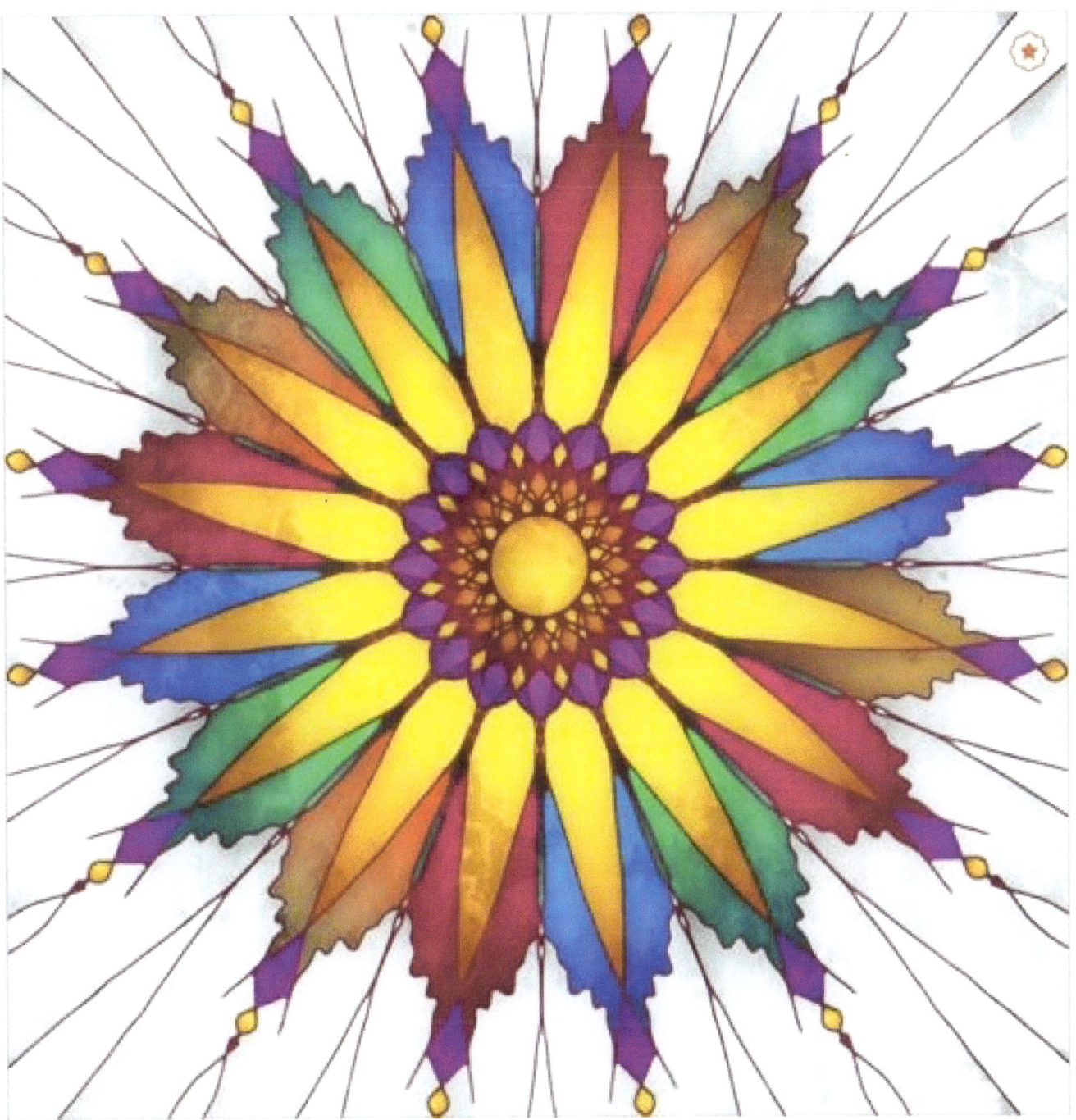

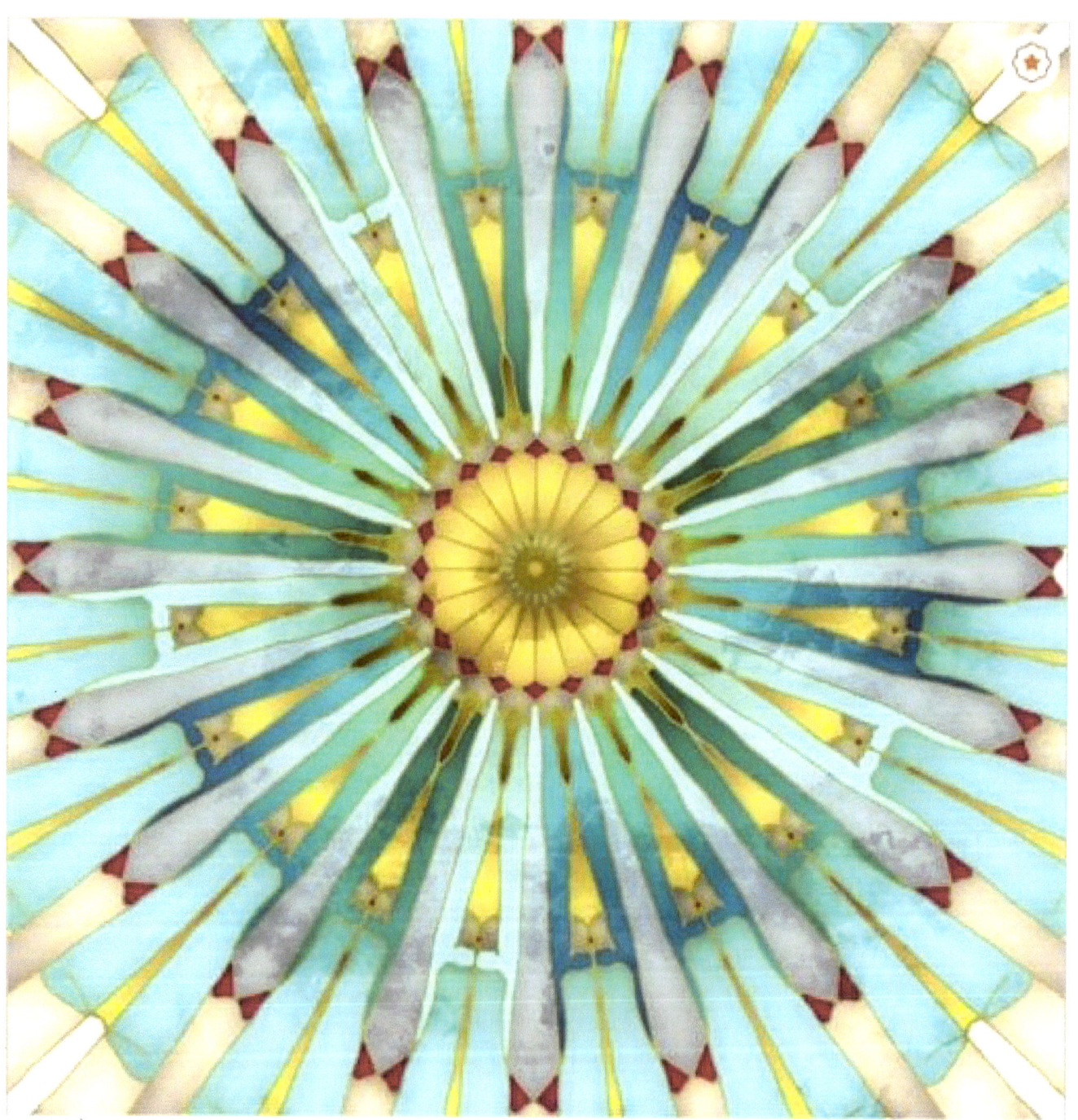

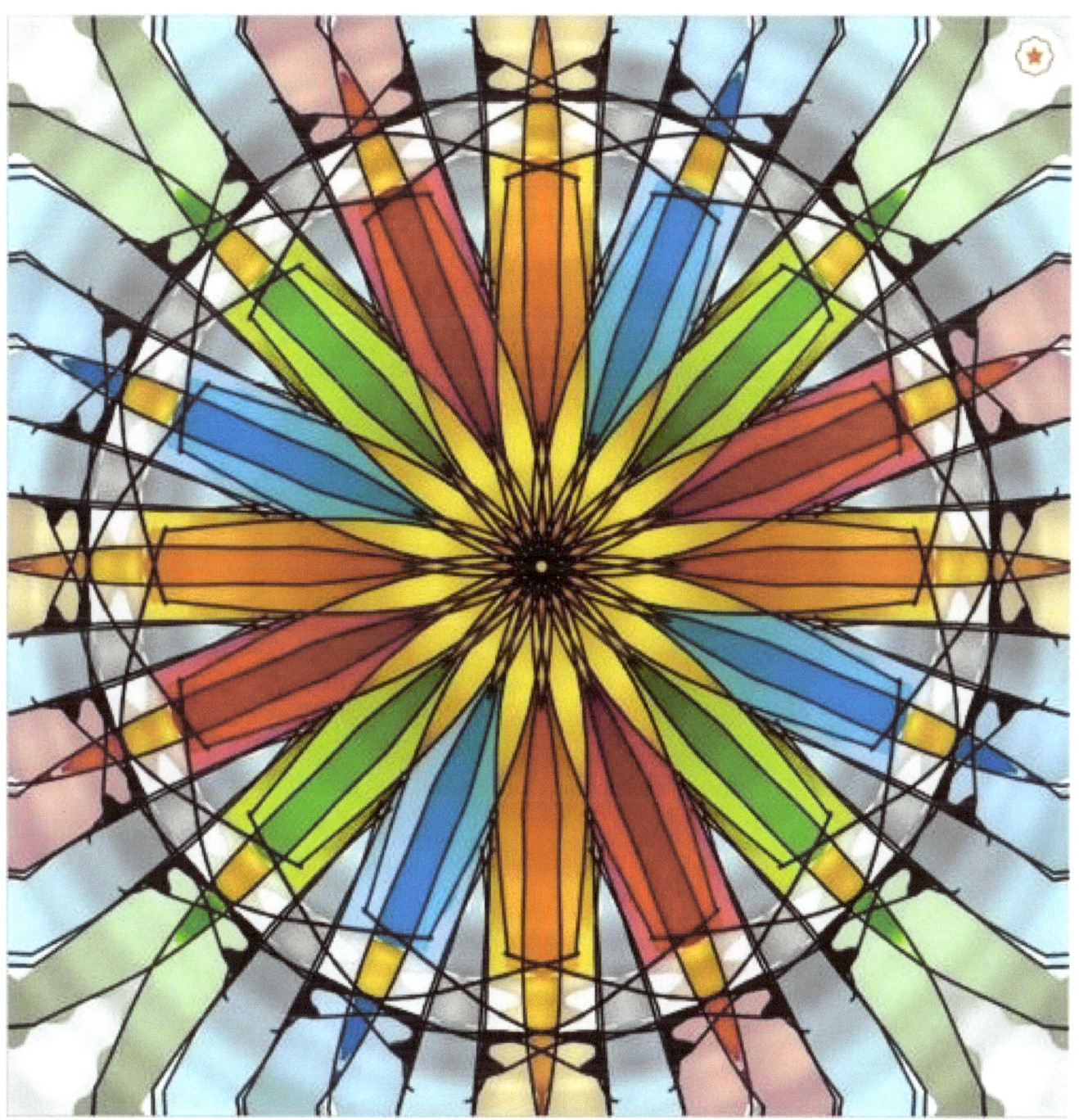

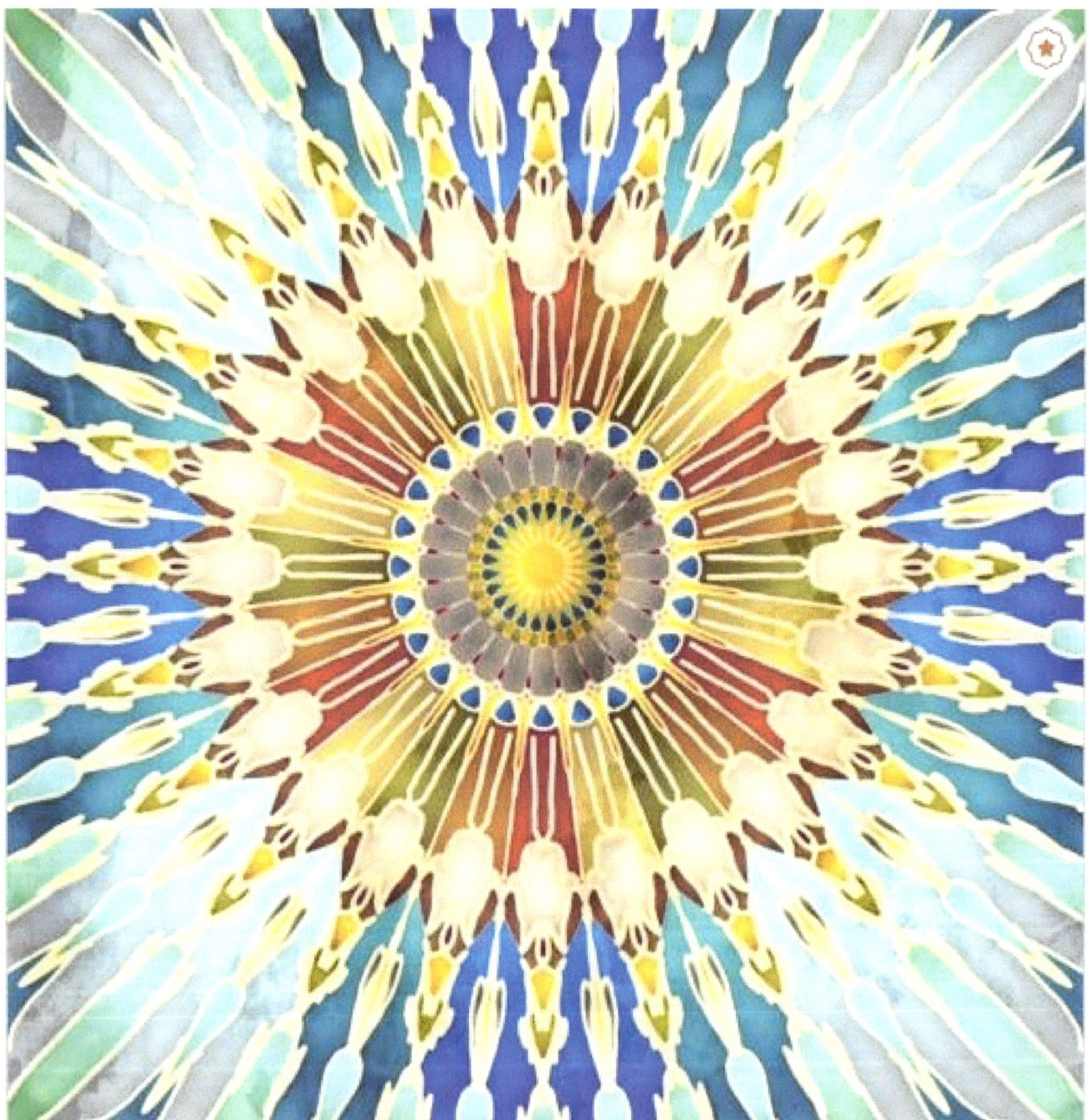

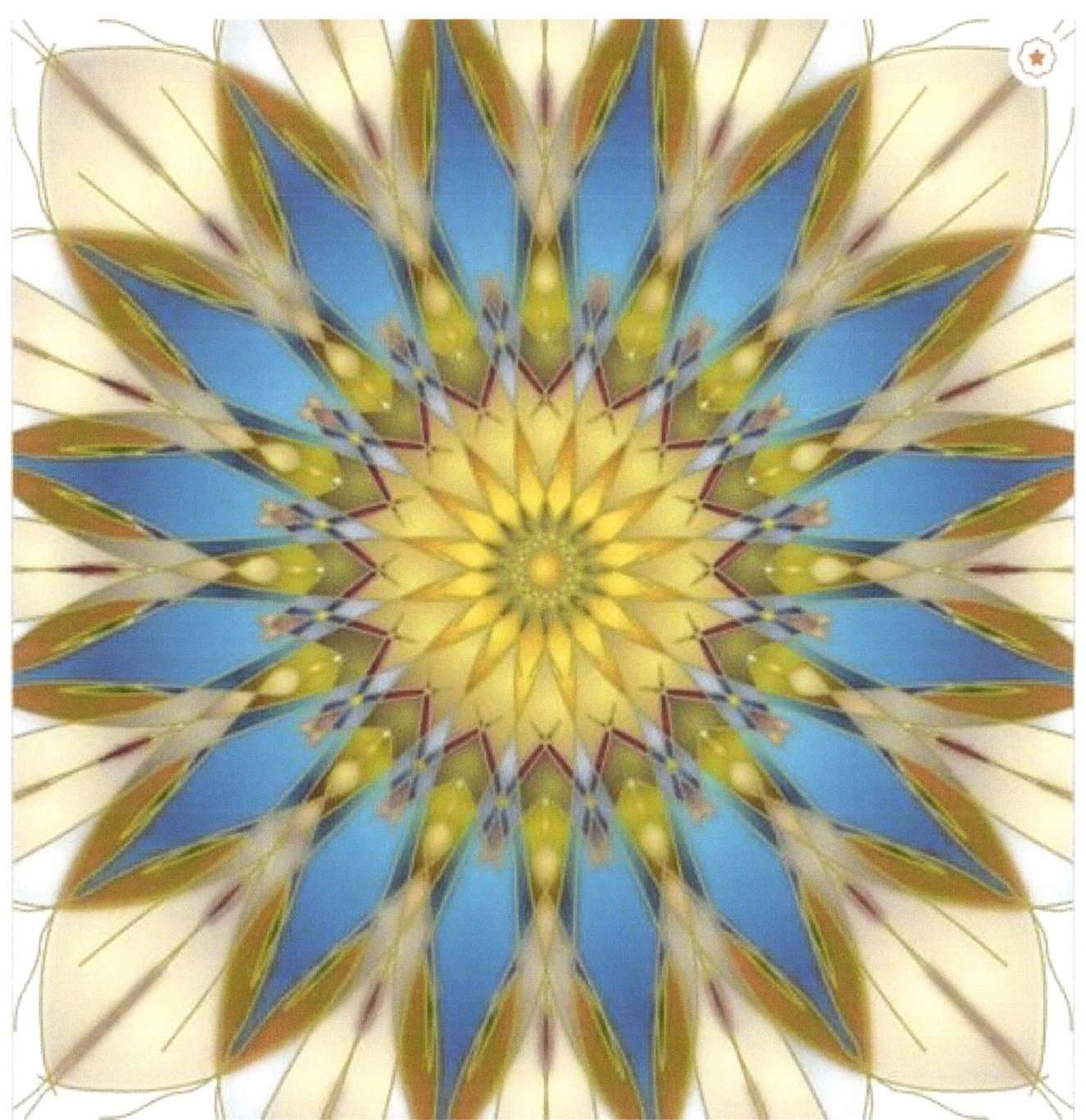

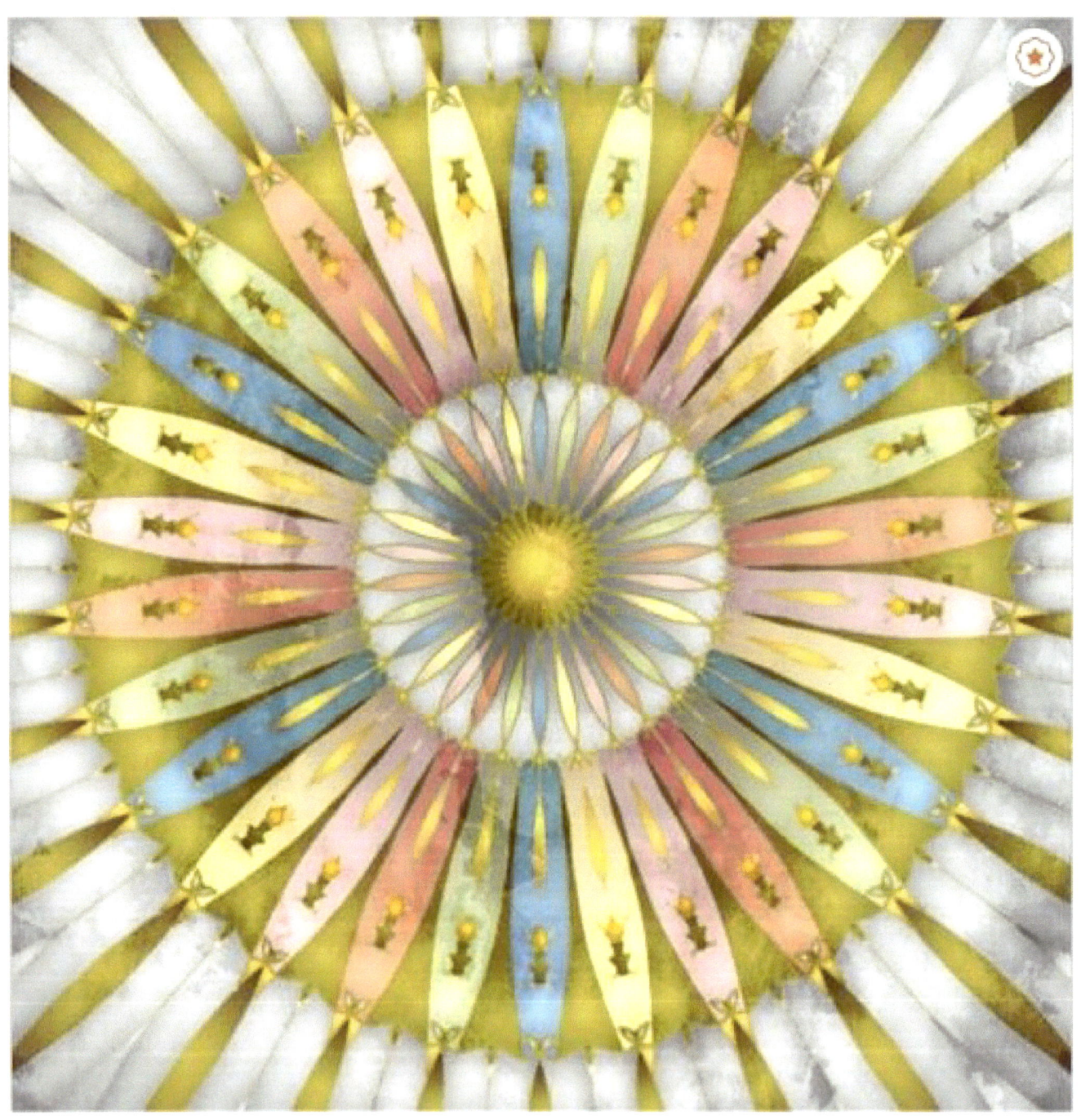

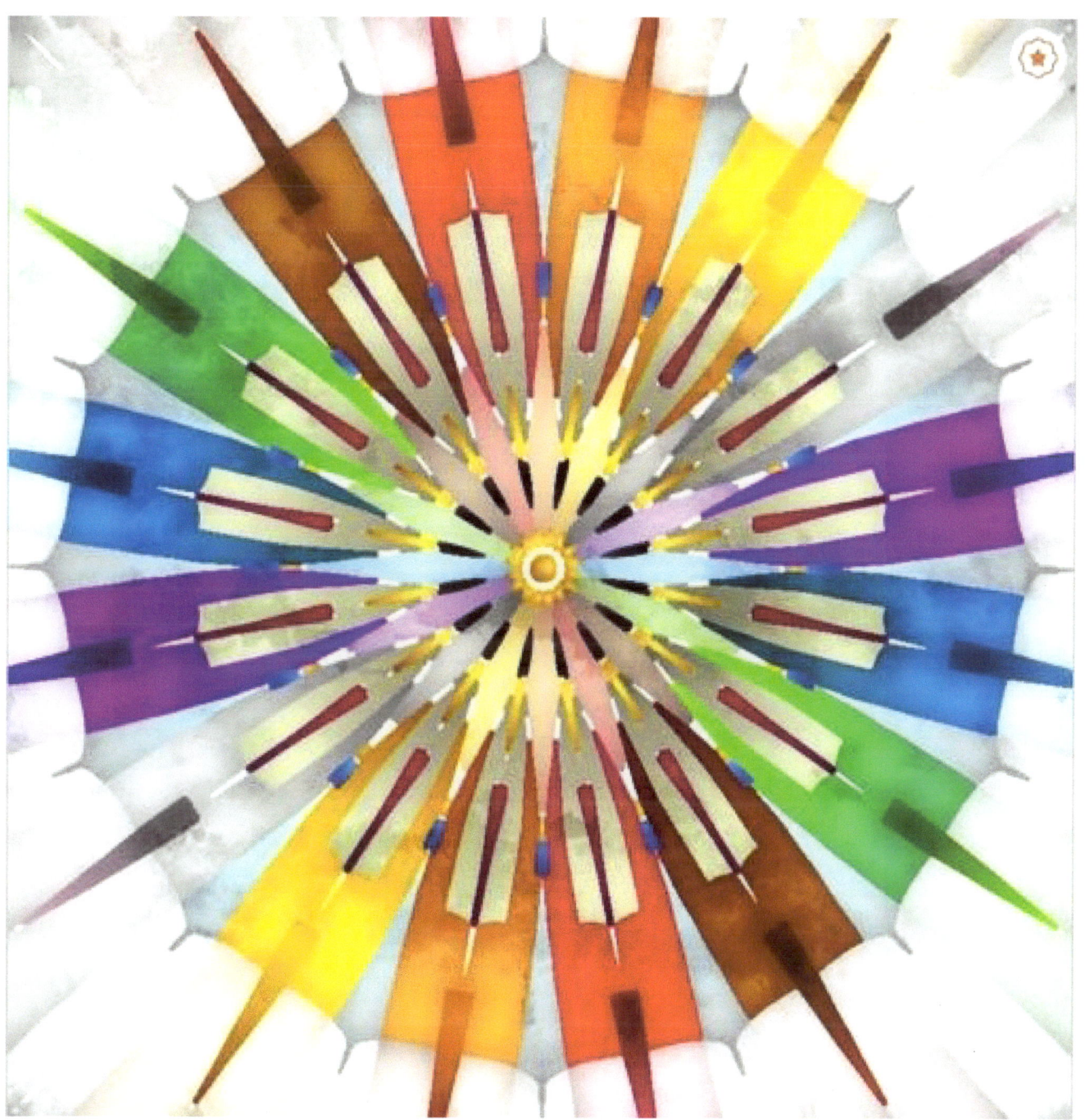

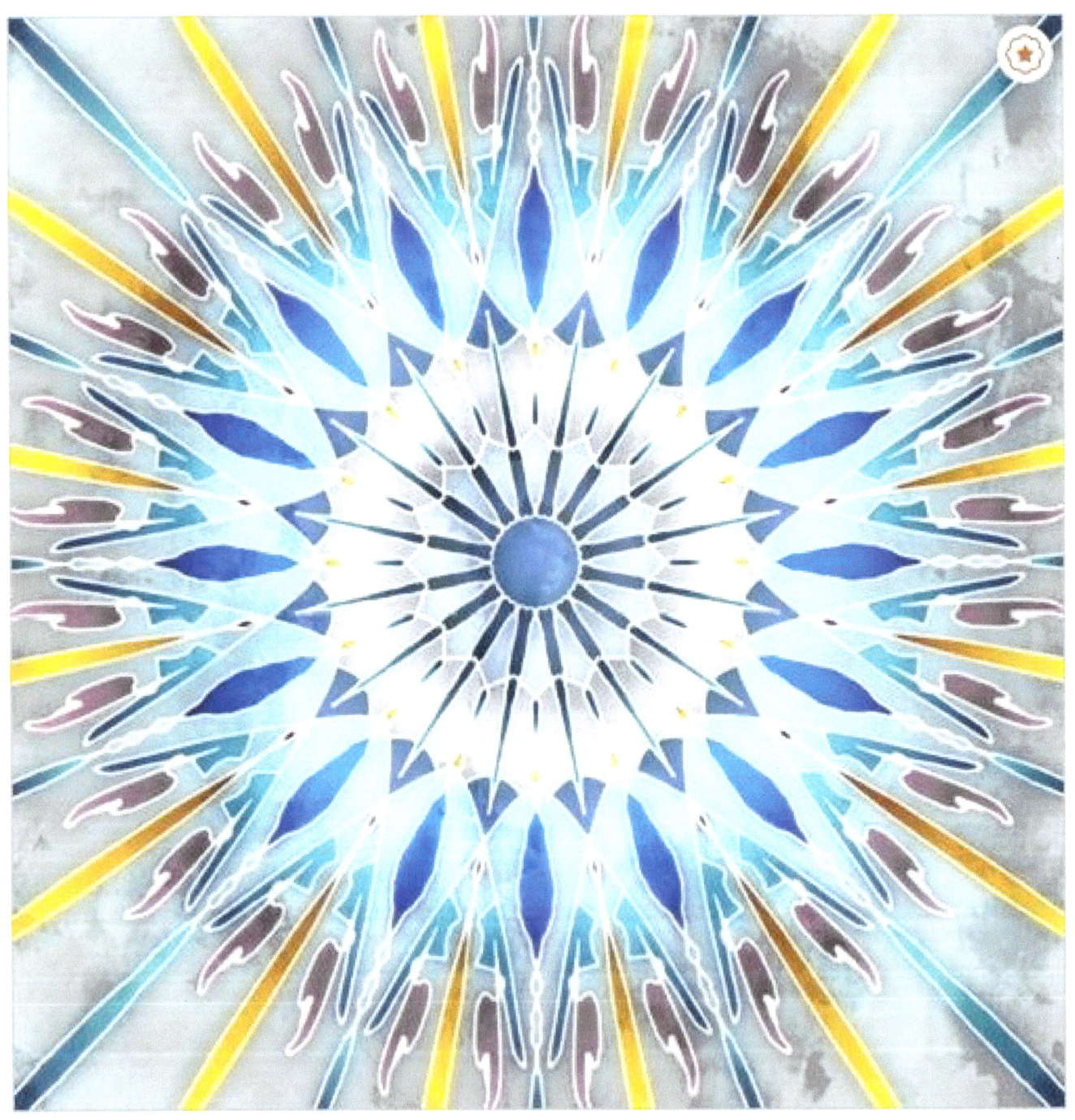

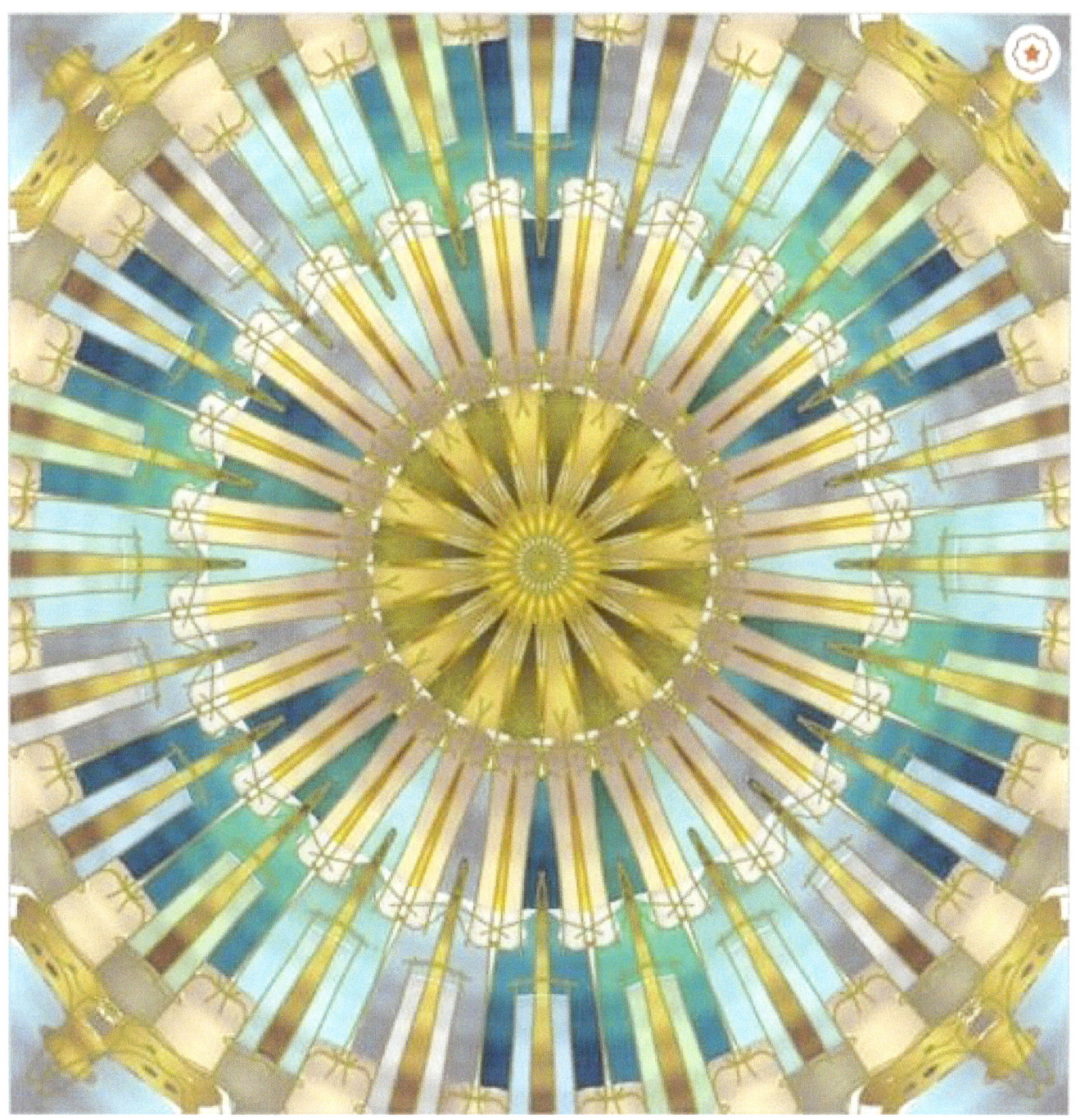

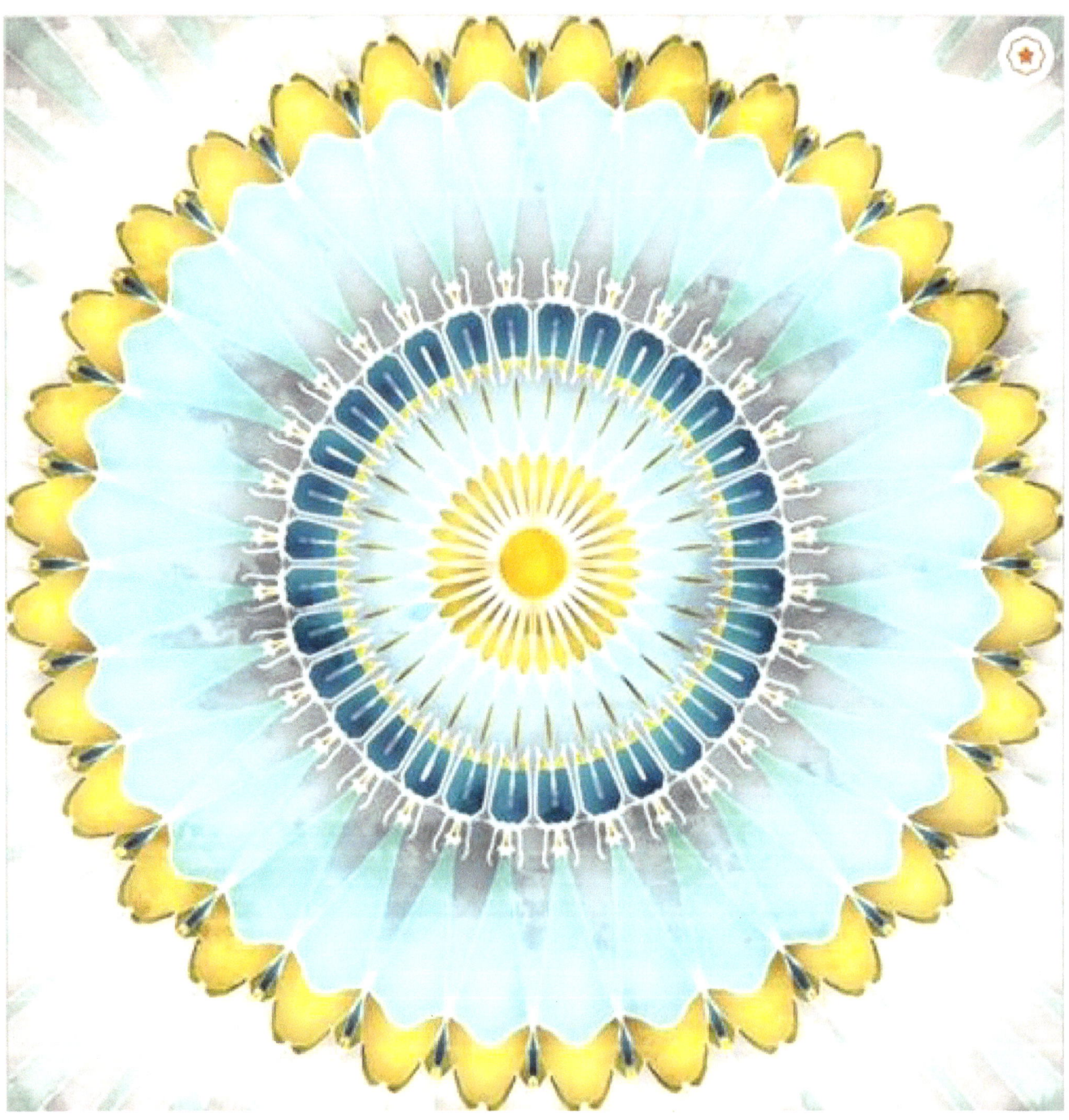

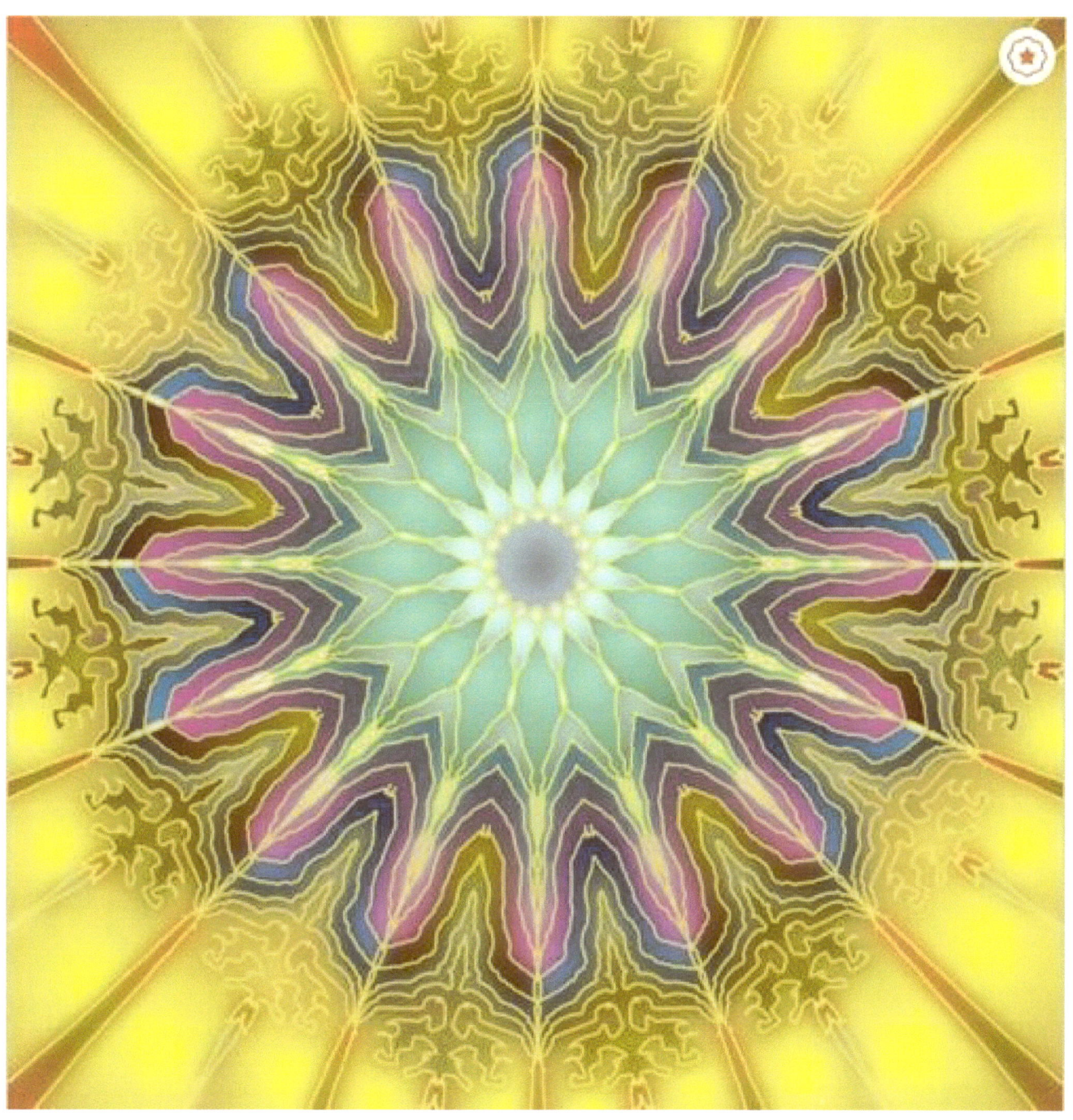

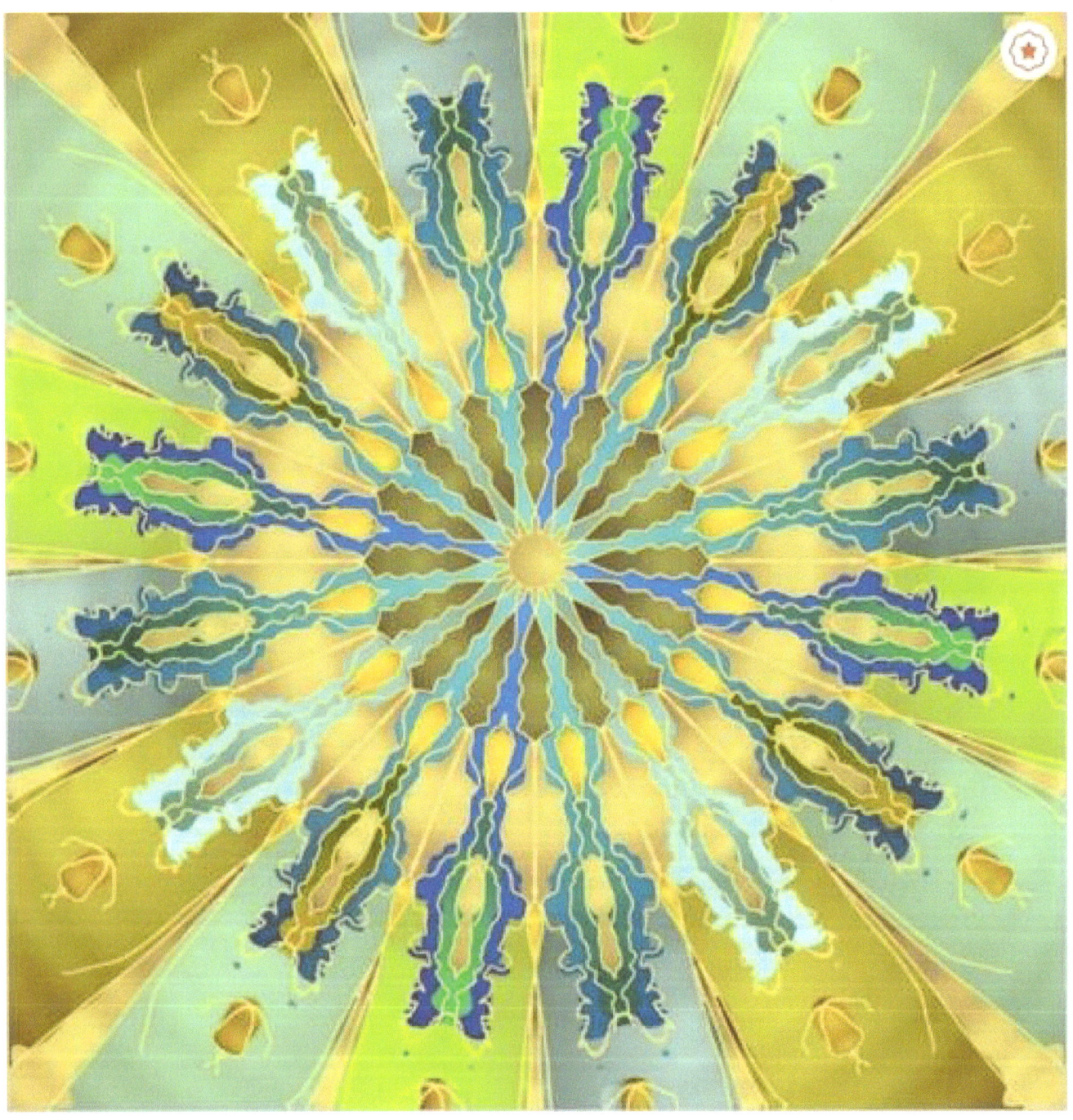

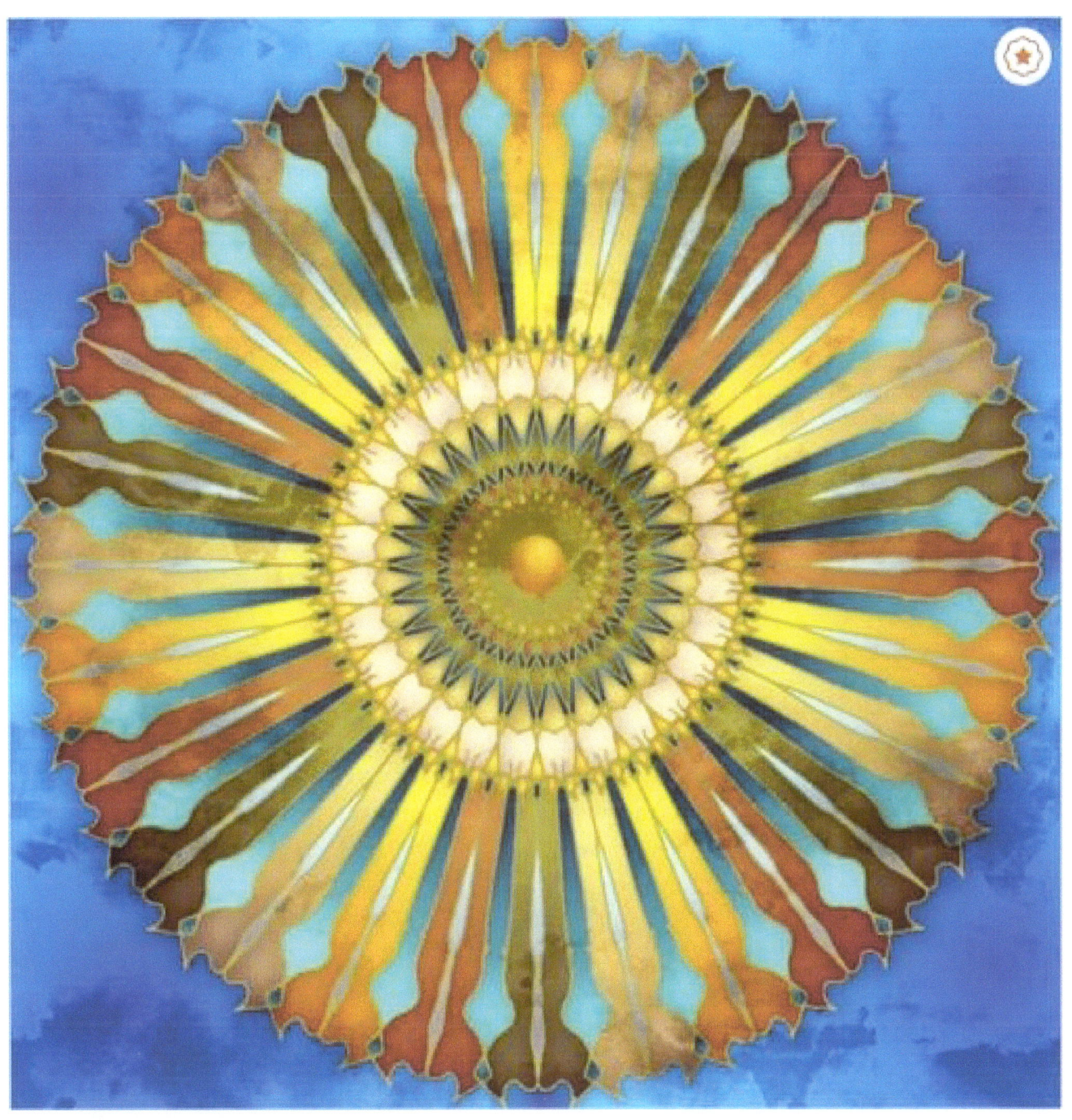

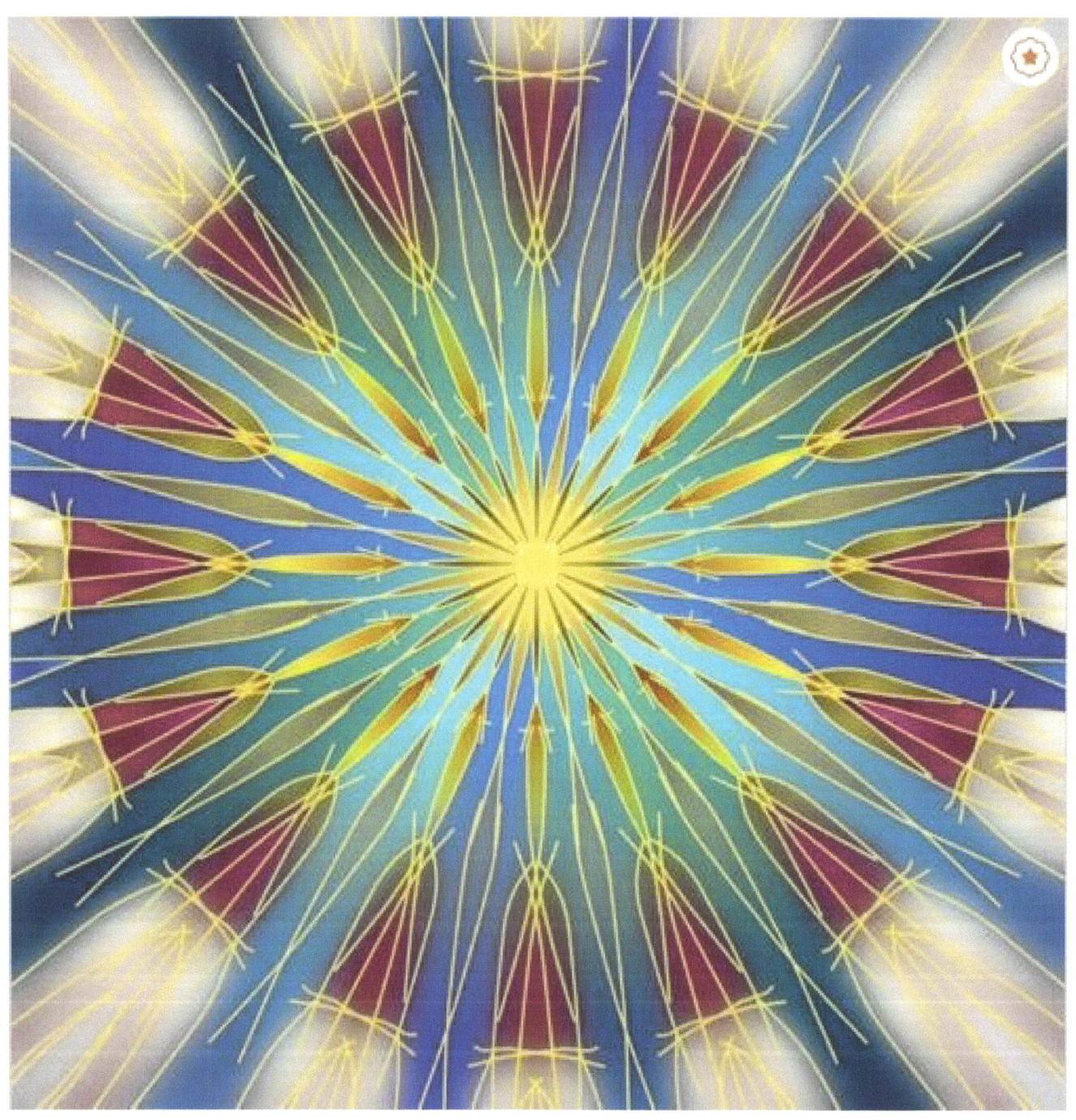

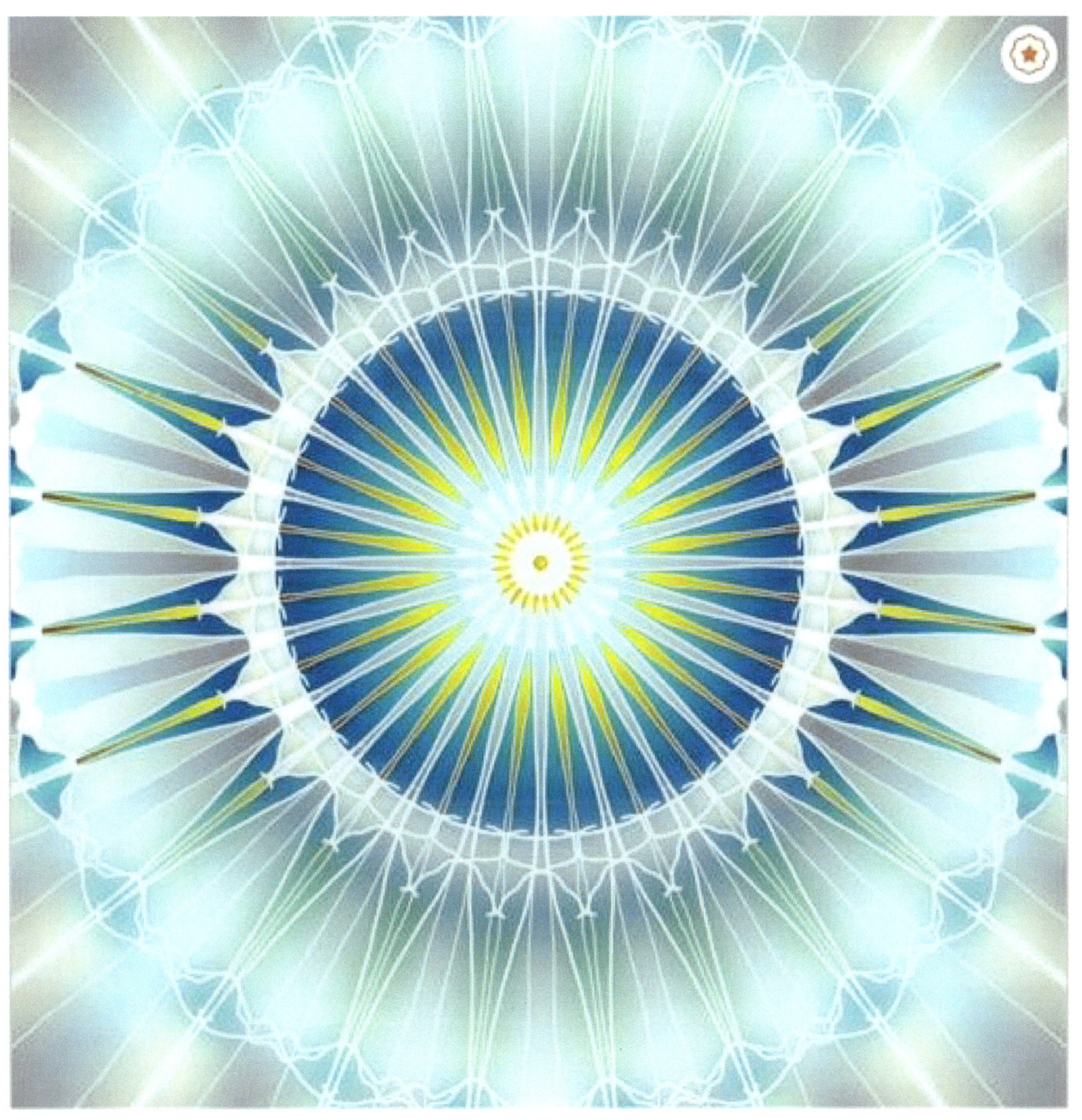

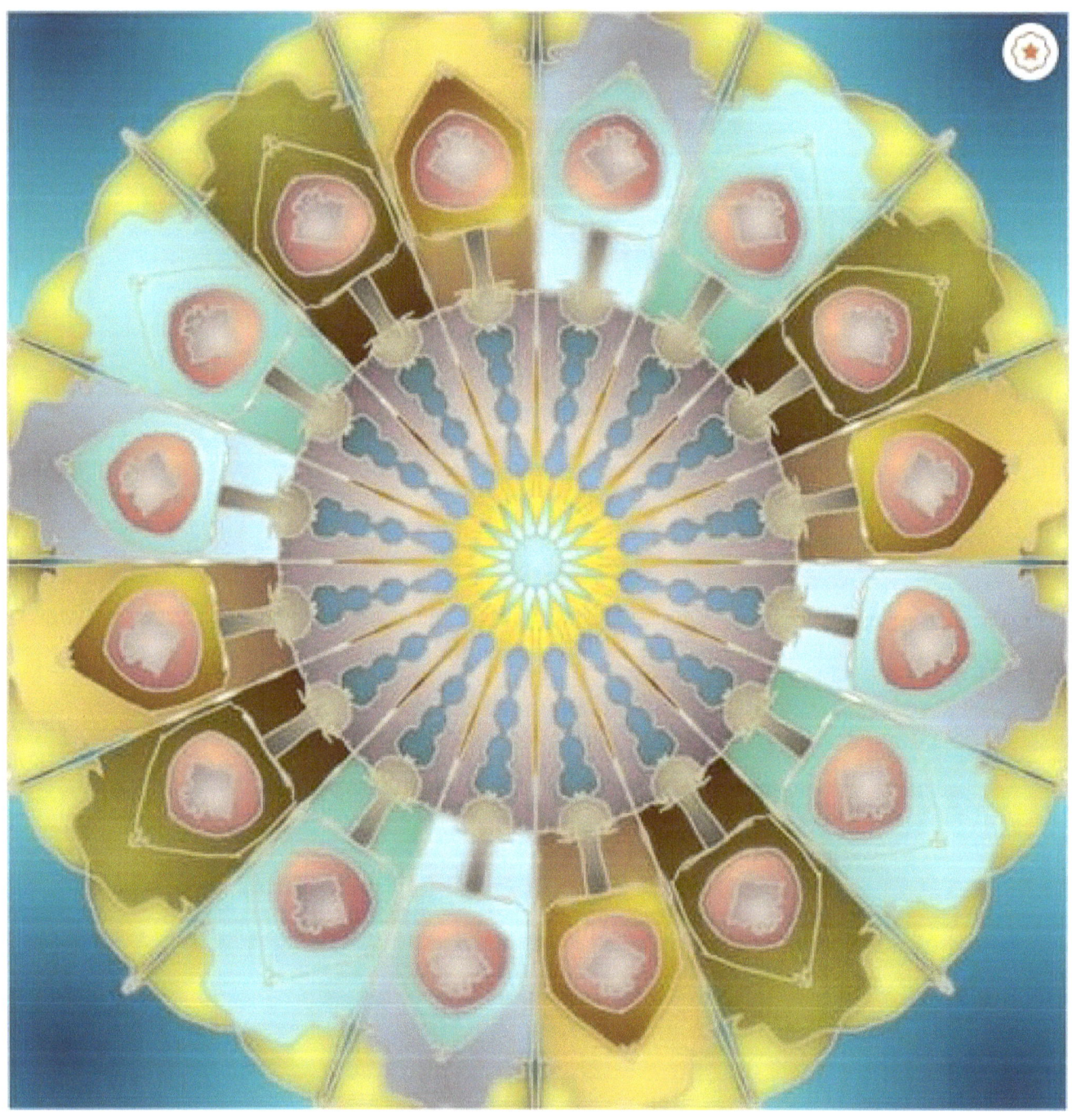

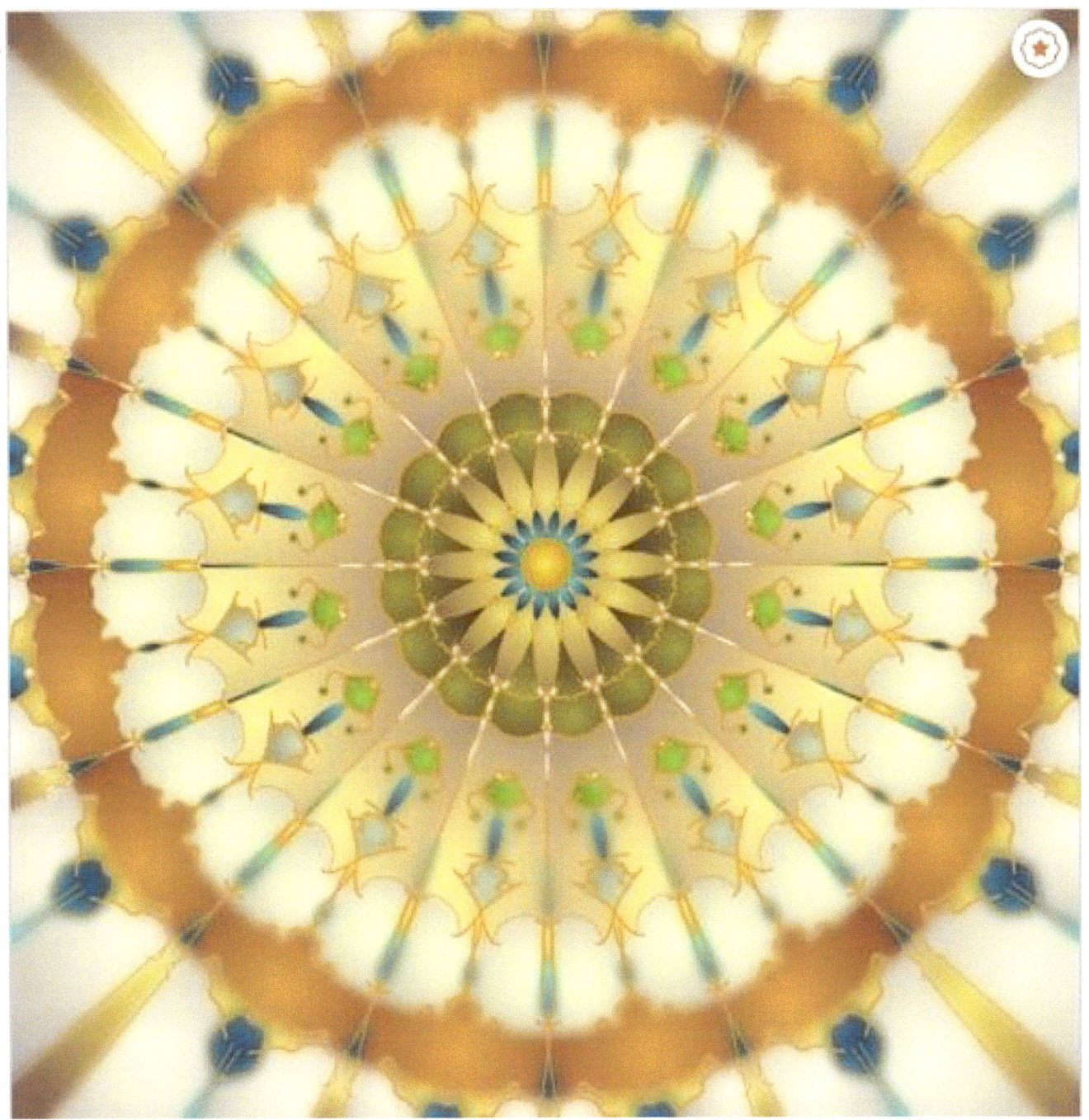

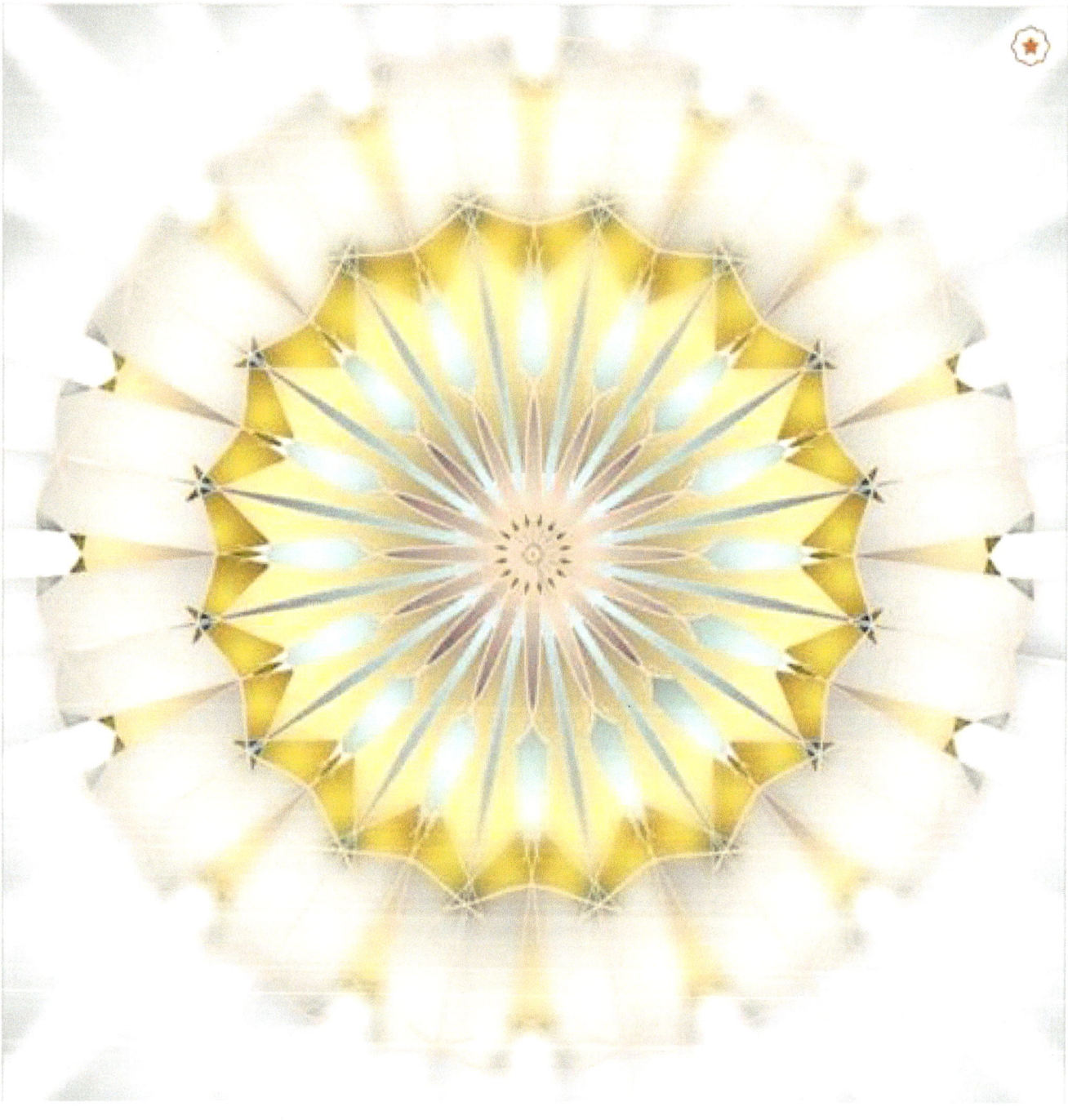

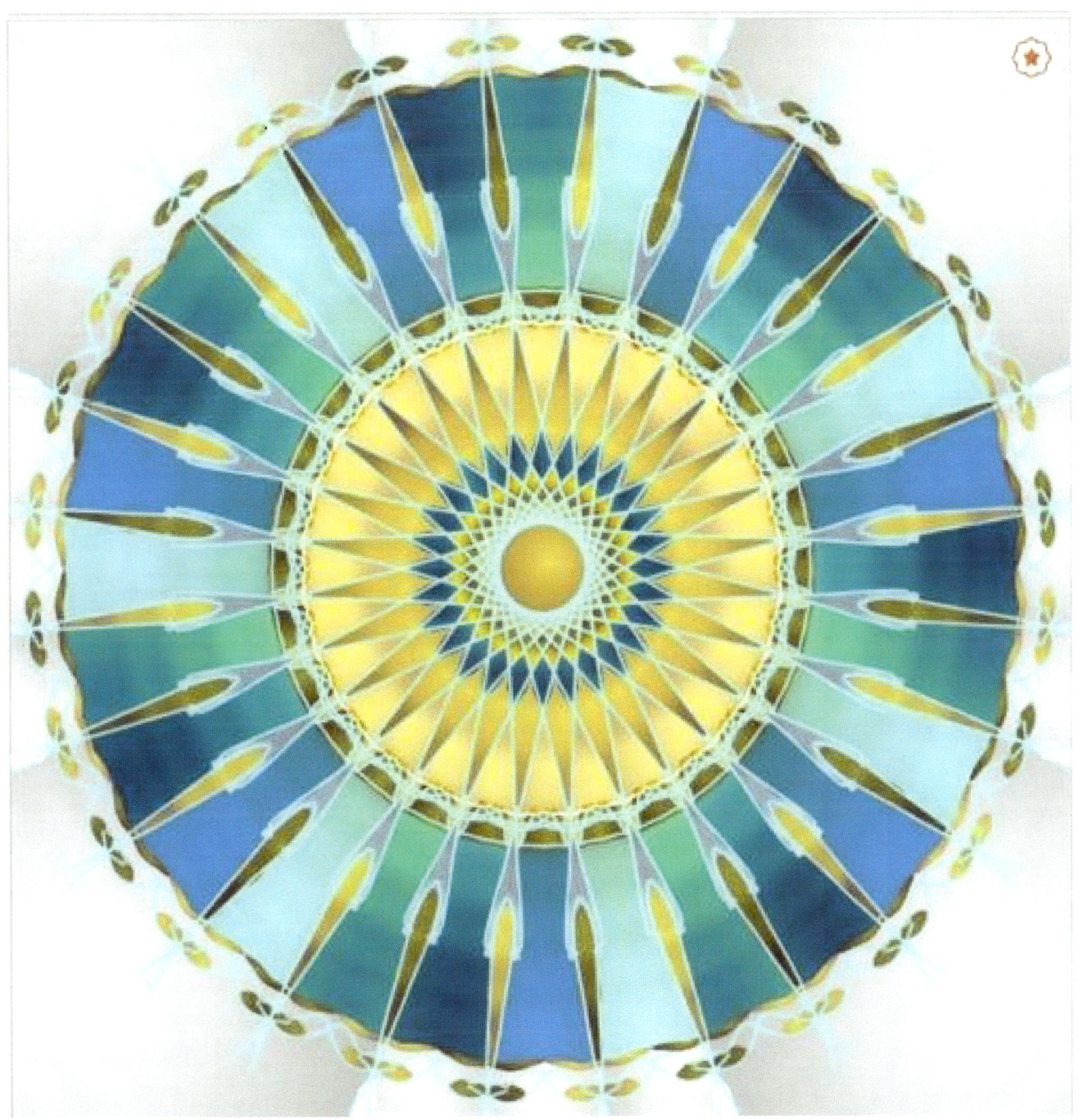

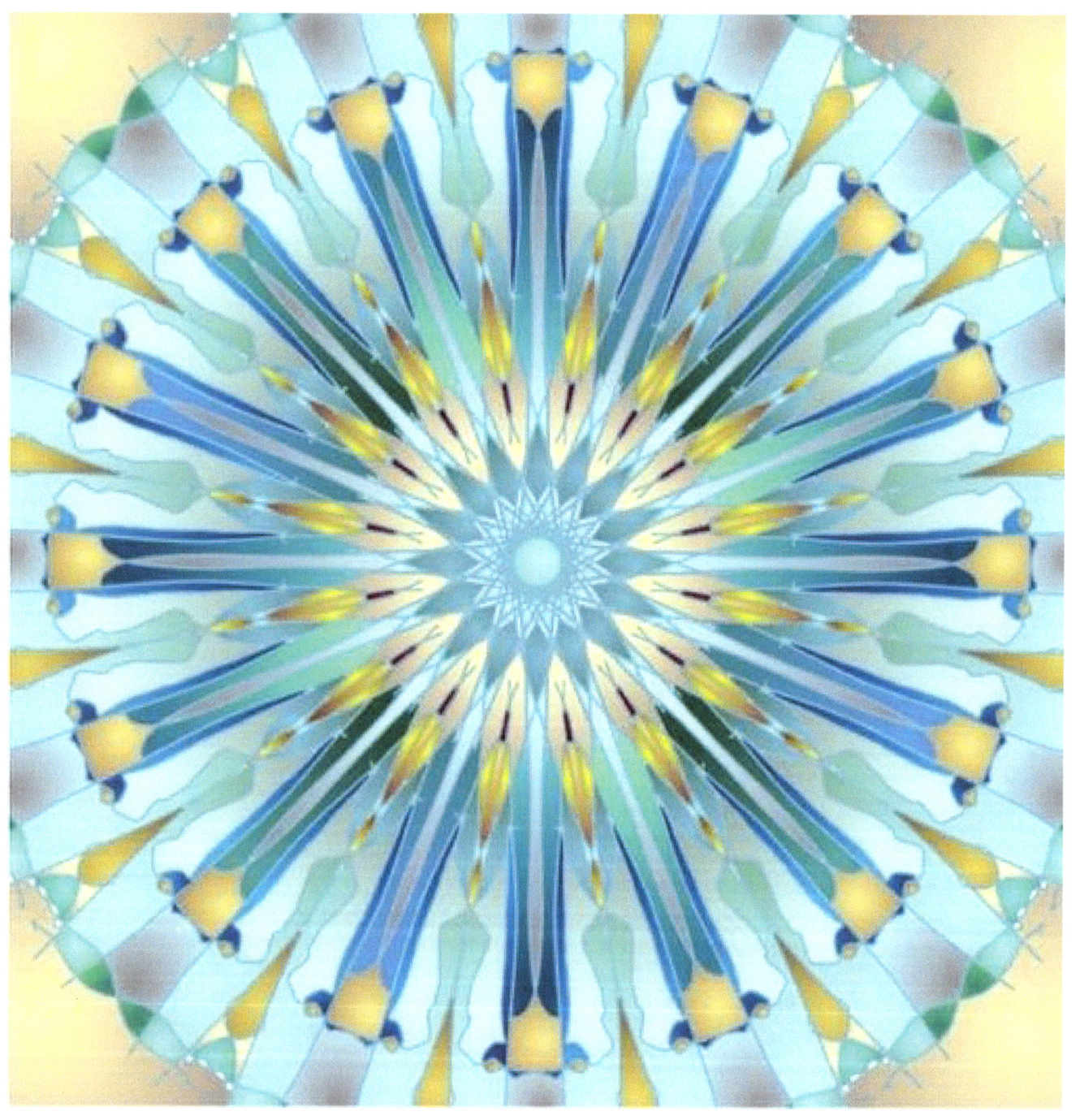

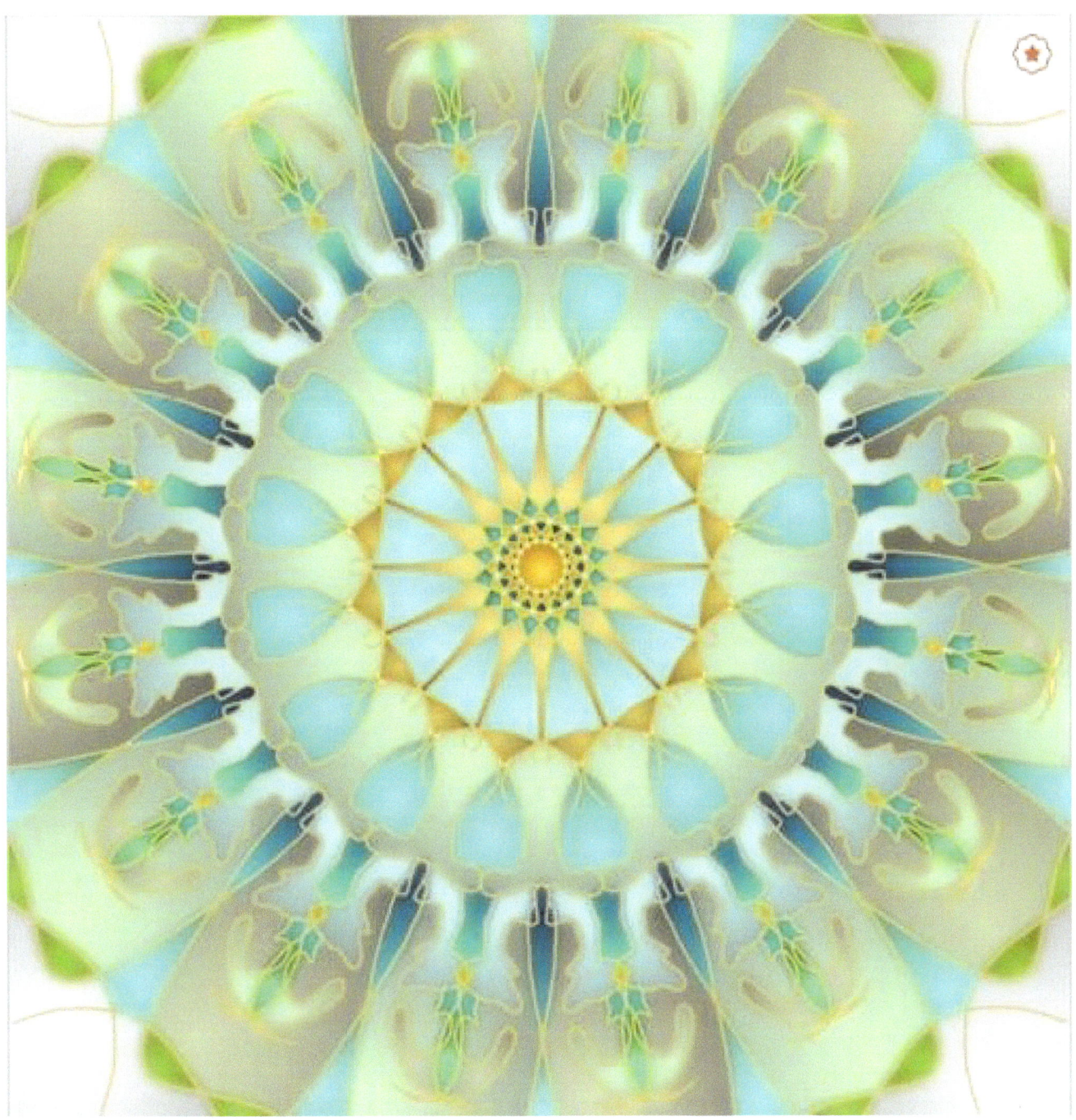

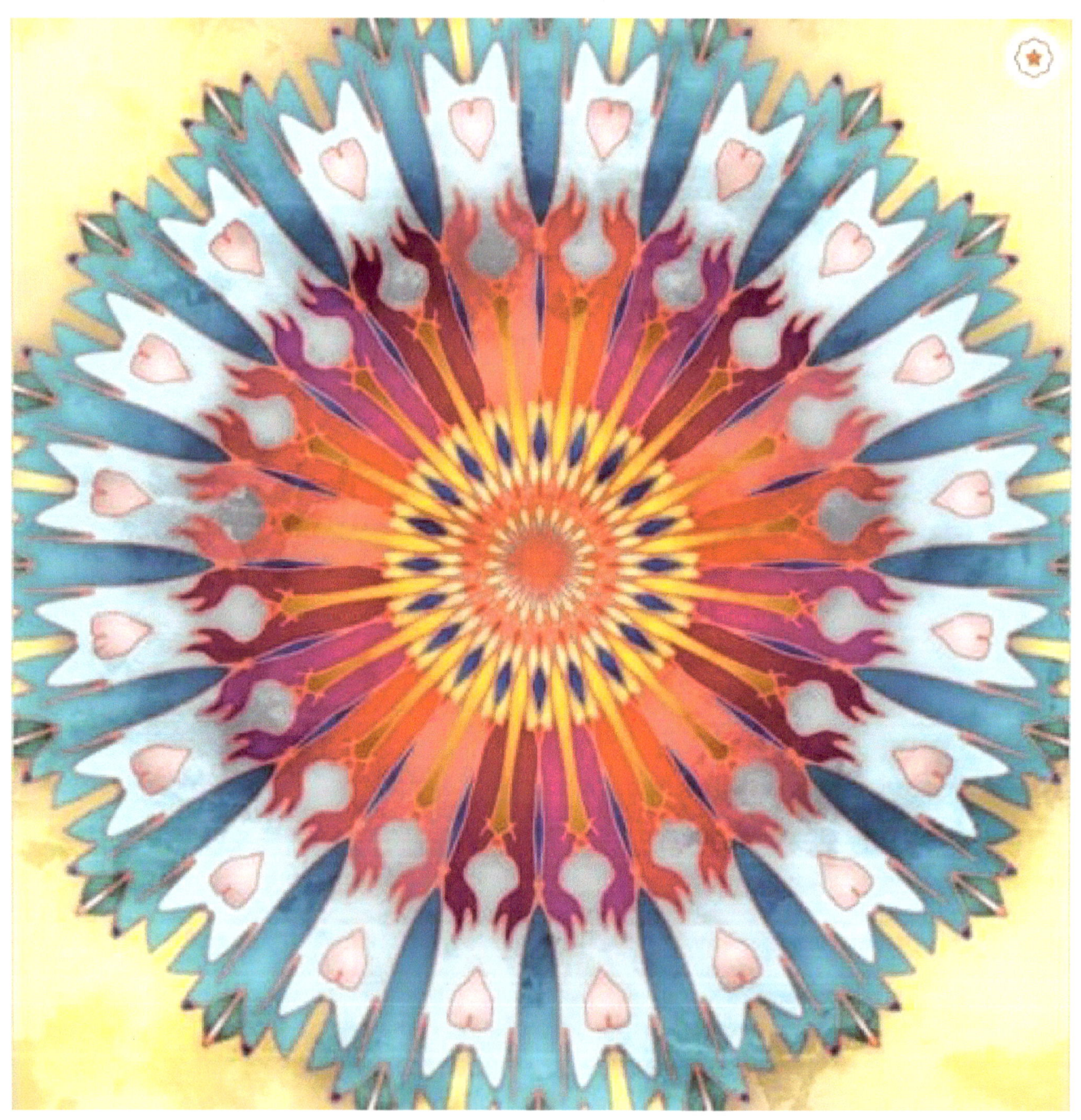

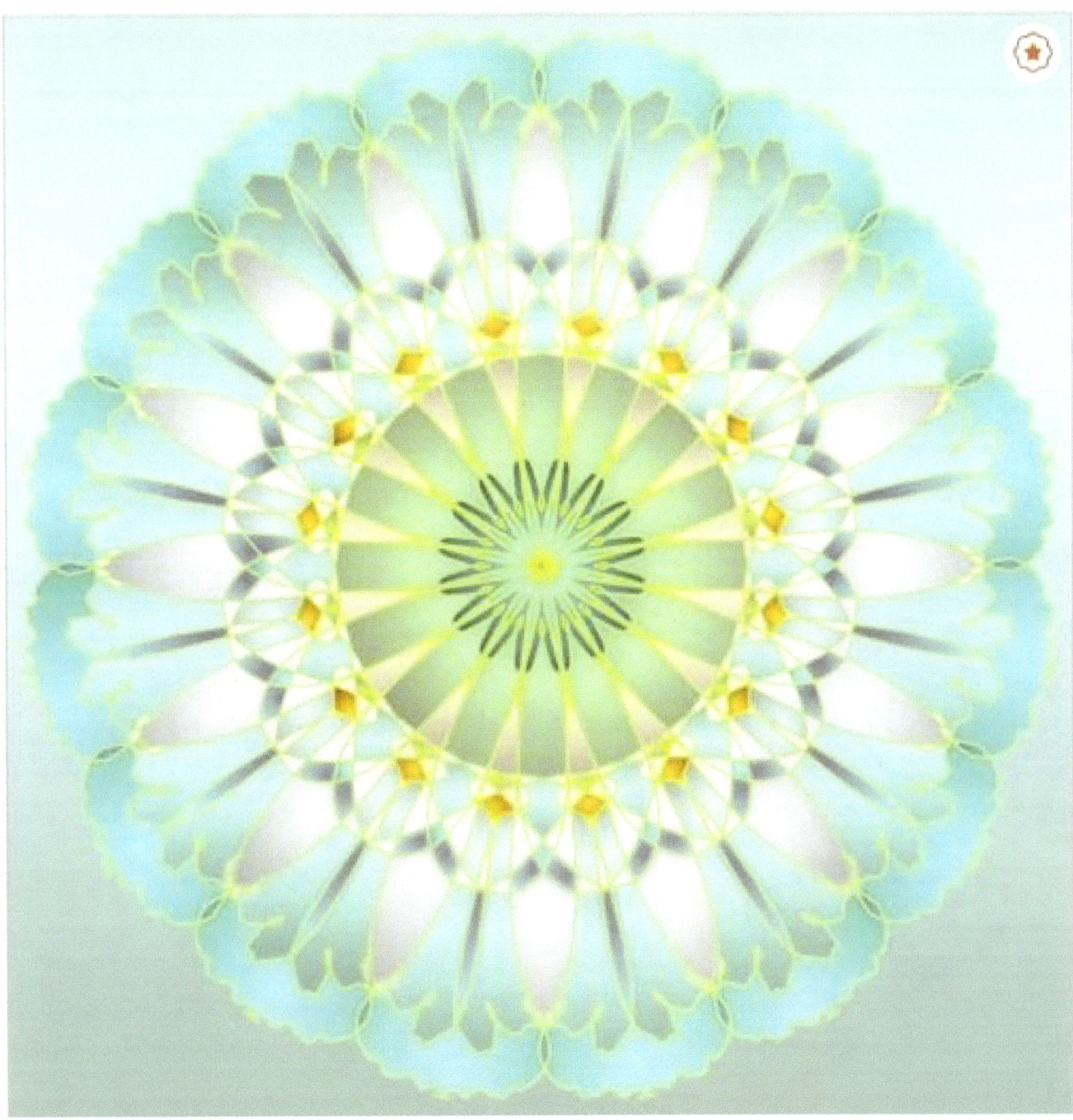

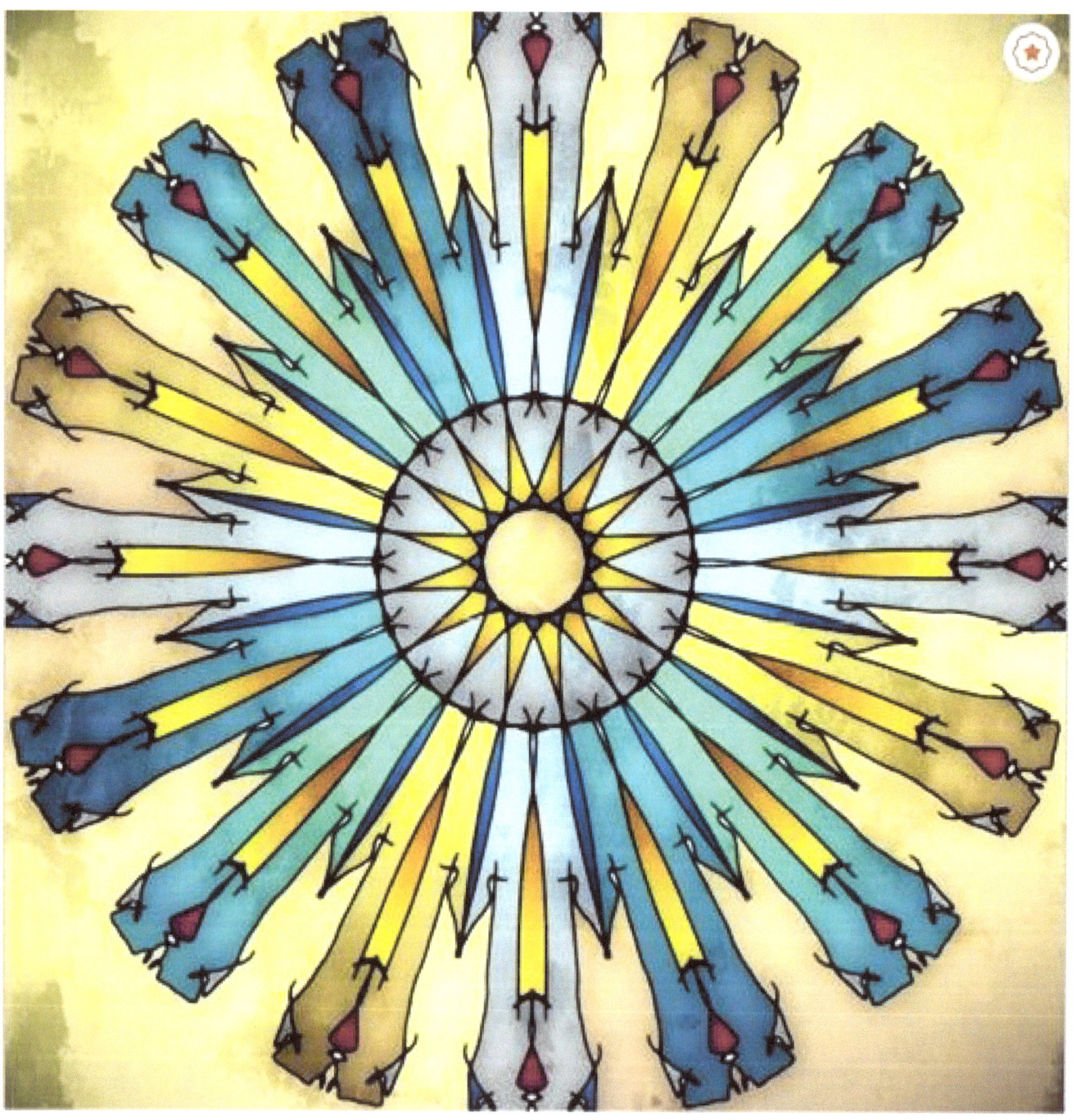

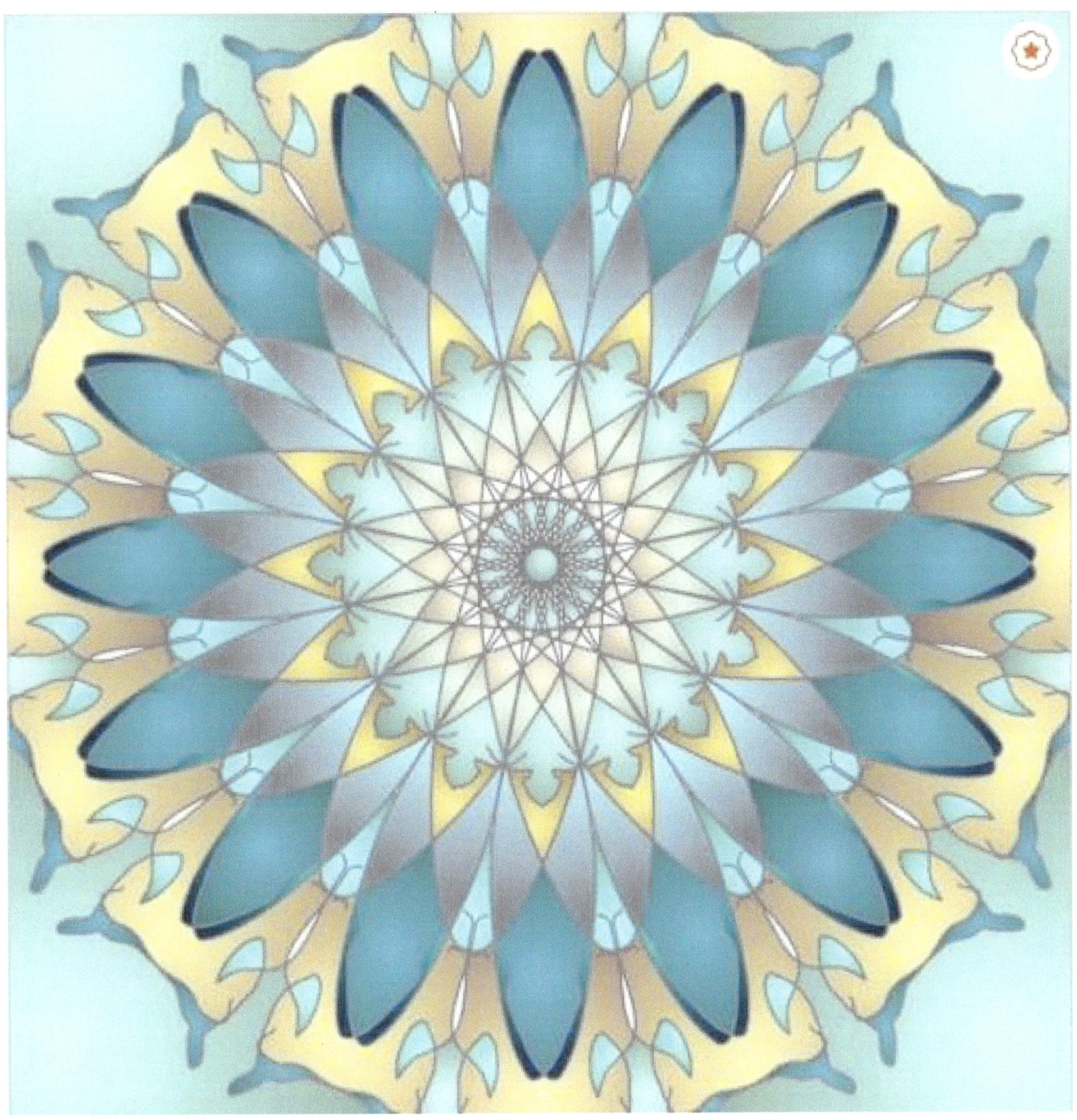

ABOUT THE AUTHOR

Jean Williams is a 62 year old Autistic woman, who spent much of her life hiding in what she called "a shell in a hole in a tunnel, underneath dark clouds." After the death of her father, and falling into a deep depression, she wondered if she wanted to continue. The concept of "feather presents" – looking for and finding each of those little gifts the world has to offer was what helped her to regain her footing, and find her way out of the tunnel. An occasional dark cloud admittedly still lingers, but she works on fighting them off, too. All of the posters in this book utilize her own photographs or artwork.

Jean has spent 30+ years in the IT industry as a Software Engineer and Database Analyst. She is happily married for over forty years, and is the mother of one daughter, and grandmother to three charming little boys.

www.ingramcontent.com/pod-product-compliance
Lightning Source LLC
Chambersburg PA
CBHW051025180526
45172CB00002B/468